it's not you, it's
CAPITALI$M

why it's time to break up
and how to move on

it's not you, it's
CAPITALI$M

why it's time to
break up and
how to move on

Malaika Jabali

illustration and design by Kayla E.

Published by
Algonquin Books of Chapel Hill
Post Office Box 2225
Chapel Hill, North Carolina 27515-2225

an imprint of Workman Publishing Co., Inc.,
a subsidiary of Hachette Book Group, Inc.
1290 Avenue of the Americas
New York, NY 10104

Printed in the United States of America.
Illustration and design by Kayla E.

The publisher is not responsible for websites (or their content)
that are not owned by the publisher.

Library of Congress Cataloging-in-Publication Data
Names: Jabali, Malaika, author.
Title: It's not you, it's capitalism : why it's time to break up and how to
move on / Malaika Jabali ; illustration and design by Kayla E..
Description: First edition. | Chapel Hill, North Carolina : Algonquin Books
of Chapel Hill, [2023] | Includes bibliographical references. | Summary:
"An illustrated guide to socialism for budding anticapitalists who know
it's time to dump their toxic ex (Capitalism) and try something finer.
Journalist Malaika Jabali debunks myths, centers forgotten socialists of
color who have shaped our world, and shows socialism is not all Marx and
Bernie Bros—it can be pretty sexy" — Provided by publisher.
Identifiers: LCCN 2023022905 | ISBN 9781643752648 (hardcover) |
ISBN 9781643755656 (ebook)
Subjects: LCSH: Socialism. | Capitalism.
Classification: LCC HX73 .J33 2023 | DDC 335.43/7—dc23/eng/20230630
LC record available at https://lccn.loc.gov/2023022905

10 9 8 7 6 5 4 3 2 1
First Edition

CONTENTS

The Break-Up

I broke up with capitalism around my junior year of college. Ever since, I've felt like the patient friend waiting for my bestie to see why she needs to break up with her toxic partner, too.

While socialism has captured mainstream attention in the US in the past decade or so, probably because of the popularity of Bernie Sanders and the Democratic Socialists of America, I didn't arrive at my anti-capitalism through electoral politics. It was through studying Black history as an undergrad that I started to see how messed up our whole system really was. Reading about how slaveholders were willing to kidnap, brand, torture, and work their labor force to near-death—oh and create a system of white supremacy to maintain their profits that still thrives today—will do that to you.

I also soaked in the words of Black revolutionaries who spoke out against capitalism, including my godfather Charles Barron, a former member of the Black Panther Party. "We keep fighting the symptoms," he is prone to say. "But capitalism is the disease."

But it wasn't until I was in grad school for social work, in the heart of the world's financial capital, that I began to think seriously about other options I'd want to settle down with. It was 2008. Absolutely nothing major happened that year, besides, y'know, the fall of Wall Street. A core memory of Gen-Xers may be the fall of the Berlin Wall and the West celebrating the end of communism. But for a lot of millennials like me, the collapse of big banks—and its repercussions for the economy and for everyday working people—was our core memory, and it made many of us a bit more critical of the country's capitalist relationship.

Those repercussions included me finishing my masters in a recession and with a crapload of student loans. I couldn't find full-time work and had a series of odd jobs. One of those was a stint as an administrative assistant for an investment manager back home in Atlanta. My job largely consisted of fielding calls from investors who were demanding a return on their investments. Some even showed up at my job to find my boss. He was never around, they never got those returns, and he was eventually charged with fraud for running a Ponzi scheme. Definitely have some loving, long-lasting impressions of capitalists from that whole situation.

That same year, I had to haggle with a mortgage servicer that was using deceptive practices to squeeze my family of money. A few years before that, a different lender targeted us with a subprime loan, and they sold our mortgage to the servicer. Like, we didn't even ask to be in this relationship! We were forced into it. The property values in our part of metro Atlanta took a nosedive, like lots of Black neighborhoods during the Great Recession. We were underwater and getting foreclosure notices even though we were making on-time payments. It took over a decade to recover—and that was mostly because a random pandemic that devastated the rest of the economy had people moving to warmer climates and rushing to buy homes in our neighborhood.

I didn't spend most of my life witnessing any sort of "compassionate" capitalism. I saw a clusterf*ck.

The world was a hot mess, and I needed to make sense of what was going on. But the stuff I read frequently seemed to miss something. I disliked how some progressive books about economic injustice and corporate malfeasance were really, really good at identifying the problems, but then concluded with something lame like, "we just need better reforms." Other books had Marxist theory down to a science, but you would never know from their narratives that there were tons of women and people of color who practiced and preached anti-capitalism, or just how much capitalism was built on slave labor and anti-Blackness. Or even how much socialism was central to the liberation movements of African, Asian, and Latin American countries fighting colonialism and imperialism. The foundational ideas of people like W. E. B. Du Bois, Kathleen Cleaver, Ella Baker, and Evo Morales are practically erased from so many visions of American socialism today.

Meanwhile, most of us outside academic and activist circles continue to think we're the ones failing at life, and not that capitalism is fundamentally flawed. Like the toxic partner we can't seem to leave, capitalism is still going strong and reeling us in with occasional gifts (here's $15 an hour and casual Fridays, happy now??). But capitalists (we'll get into who they are later) have been getting way more out of this relationship than the rest of us.

After you read the next ten chapters, I hope that you'll be ready to break up and move the hell on from this monster, and that you can convince your friends and your boomer parents and your day-trading uncles to do the same.

For the first three chapters of the book, I lay the groundwork with basic definitions of capitalism and socialism and how they intersect with race. In the following chapters, I share more specifics of how capitalism Fs us over: from housing and healthcare to our jobs, student loans, and the whole concept of American democracy—and this minor aspect of our lives: the entire planet we live on. Especially in the final chapter, but throughout the entire book, we'll talk about what we can do with all this information, how we can make life better for everyone we know and love, with insight from contemporary socialist luminaries.

This book isn't just about making you angry and depressed by my enumerating of unsolvable problems. I mean, it will probably do that a little bit (sorry!!), but I hope it will also encourage you to join other people in a collective struggle to leave the sh*t world we inherited behind. Let capitalism be that ex who's resigned to silently creep on your Instagram stories and rant about you to their friends while they watch you prosper with the new boo. ✊🏽

1

Capitali$m the Catfish

"THIS IS A CAPITALIST SOCIETY.
IT'S BUILT ON INEQUALITY AND AVARICE."
—KATHLEEN CLEAVER

You remember the start of your friend's relationship. It seemed like they were being love-bombed—completely bombarded with attention and promises of a fairytale future. But you decided to let it play out. Their bae was saying all the right things at the beginning, until little by little, you notice inconsistencies. Your friend keeps holding on to those empty promises, hoping to capture the flicker of contentment they felt at the beginning. But clearly there has been no delivery on those promises, and the whole thing blows up, full drama.

A few days—and supportive texts from you and emotional FaceTimes, also with you—later, you see the fighting couple posted up on the 'gram. "What's understood doesn't need to be explained," they caption with one of those corny joint posts that shows up on the feeds of each of their followers. Back like they never left.

You're three seconds away from cussing them out in the group chat. But instead, you just tell them you'll be there for them regardless of their choices. Eventually they'll see how doomed it is, on their own, right? Right??

The toxic partner in this sad tale isn't the hot girl (or guy) covered with red flags. It's capitalism.

We've been told this is the only system that could possibly work for us. Maybe you heard that capitalism is never going away, it's the only system we know, and we've had it for so long, like the significant other we should probably live without but can't seem to leave. This is the system of prosperity and freedom!! And of course, we're all a little bit of hustle and a stroke of luck away from being the next Jeff Bezos.

Perhaps you (or your friend) have gotten a few make-up gifts from the relationship. You might finally have a well-paid job with healthcare and a 401(k), you bought that expensive air fryer you've been eyeing, and your parents are feeling like that degree paid off, so maybe you and capitalism are soulmates after all.

But imagine that things could actually be better. Think about what you've probably had to endure to get to this point of the relationship. Maybe you have a job with super intense hours, or you work multiple jobs. It took years to pay off thousands of dollars (or hundreds of thousands of dollars) of debt to get that job. You're tired and get more excited about dryer balls than clocking in.

But instead of being told that this relative lifelessness is how capitalism works, we've been convinced that we're just not trying hard enough in the relationship. We need to hustle more, sacrifice more hours and more time, find more streams of income, and we'll finally see how good our lives can be. You're doing everything you can to make this relationship work. But I can assure you, it's not you, it's capitalism.

So it's time to have an honest conversation about what capitalism is doing to us. For most of us, we have a one-sided, friends-with-(occasional)-benefits situation; not a life partner.

If you're already reading this book, you might be the patient friend in the group chat trying to convince your homies, or your family, that we need to start branching out and looking for a better alternative. This book is a guide to help you out with this.

If you're the one who needs convincing, this book is to help you avoid further heartbreak. A lot of us have seen what capitalism has done to people (and the planet!), and I just want us to do better. To understand why we should break up and move on,

it's important to get some background. You know how some friends turn into a CIA agent when they're trying to get intel on someone before their first date? I'm going to be that friend for you, before you fully commit to capitalism. Spoiler alert: It's catfishing you.

what is capitali$m?

The short answer is that capitalism is a system in which a comparatively small number of people profit off of the labor of many workers.

A capitalist is someone who hires these workers in order to profit primarily from their labor and who owns the resources workers use to produce goods and services for them, so that an individual worker does not have the power to independently produce anything or to control their working conditions. These resources could be land, raw material (say, cotton or oil), or technology.

That's capitalism in a nutshell. The rest of this chapter (and the book) is dedicated to giving you the long answer, with examples from really smart people in different countries (and not just European ones!) who have assessed capitalism's ruthless development. But given that the United States is peak capitalist and pretends that even basic things like free public healthcare are radical, we're going to focus a lot on the US.

CAPITA

Here's how some socialists and other anti-capitalists

"[Capitalism] needs a middle class to function smoothly. It doesn't need equality. What it needs is inequality. It needs a certain number of people at the elite level, a certain number of people in the middle level, and the rest of the people scrambling and hoping they could get there, all following the same zealous commitment to making money."

... **Kathleen Cleaver**

"In the current capitalist world that we live in there can be no ethical relationship that capitalism has to human beings and the non-human world. [C]apitalism will always invent new frontiers and new ways of privatizing life and we should never underestimate its cunning and its dynamic ability."

Nick Estes ·····

LI$M IS

of color in the United States characterize capitali$m:

"We've got to figure out a way to do away with this brutal capitalism that we have in the United States, where you have 10 percent of the wealthy owning most of the wealth."

Dolores Huerta

"I am convinced that capitalism has seen its best days in America, and not only in America, but in the entire world. It is a well-known fact that no social institution can survive when it has outlived its usefulness. This, capitalism has done. It has failed to meet the needs of the masses."

Martin Luther King, Jr.

This isn't what we hear from capitalists, though. They sweet-talk us into believing it's about prosperity! Mom-and-pop shops! And freedom! Of course the ones who benefit most from the relationship bombard us with this rhetoric. Meanwhile, they're scamming us out of thousands, if not hundreds of thousands, of dollars across our lifetimes. Even when you finally see them for what they are, you've been sucked into the fake vision they created for you. You don't want to believe it's not real. The perfect catfish.

capitali$m depends on inequality

Capitalists love to tell us about all the great things the system encourages: innovation, hustle, and wealth for hard workers. Putting aside the fact that government funding, not capitalism, has sparked much of America's technology and creativity, focusing on these positive developments ignores the really, really bad reality on the ground.

For centuries, America's capitalists have worked to structure society so that it most benefits them. For instance, they lobby for policies to make sure there are few limits on the wealth they can accumulate, from laws minimizing union power so workers can't bargain for better benefits and wages, to trade deals that allow capitalists to seek cheaper labor in developing countries, to fighting against a $15 federal minimum wage. This results in a completely skewed distribution of the country's wealth and income.

Despite all the "innovation" of capitalism, capitalists have somehow failed to evolve from their reliance on inequality. In fact, it just keeps getting worse. In the 1700s, when the US had an economy built on the labor of literal enslaved people who had no income, income inequality then was still not as bad as it is today. Mind. Blown.

Even if you look at the so-called golden age of American capitalism, from 1950 to 1970, history shows this was a rare window of relative prosperity, compared to the eras that preceded it and the decades since. And, hello: Black Americans and other people of color were catching hell in that "golden age"—economically and politically—so that "relative" is very relative.

Now what does capitalism look like for us in
the United States today? As you might guess,

it sucks.

In 2021, there was about $136 trillion in wealth in America.

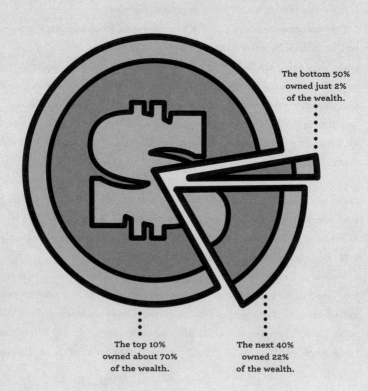

The bottom 50%
owned just 2%
of the wealth.

The top 10%
owned about 70%
of the wealth.

The next 40%
owned 22%
of the wealth.

Rich people just keep making more money...

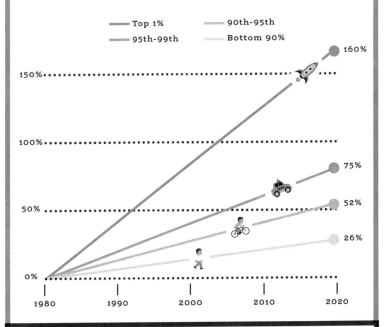

1979-2019

Legend:
- Top 1%
- 95th-99th
- 90th-95th
- Bottom 90%

Chart values:
- 160%
- 150%
- 100%
- 75%
- 52%
- 50%
- 26%
- 0%

X-axis: 1980, 1990, 2000, 2010, 2020

The top 1.0 percent of earners are now paid 160.3 percent more than they were in 1979. (Those in the top 0.1 percent had more than double that wage growth, up 345.2 percent since 1979.)

Meanwhile, wages for the bottom 90 percent only grew 26 percent in that time.

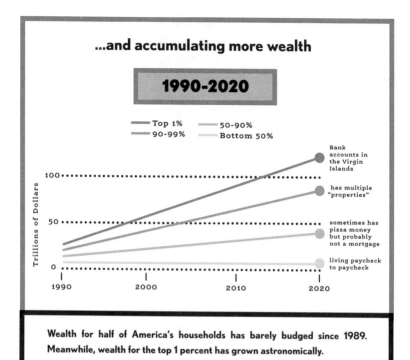

...and accumulating more wealth

1990-2020

Top 1% 50-90%
90-99% Bottom 50%

Bank accounts in the Virgin Islands

has multiple "properties"

sometimes has pizza money but probably not a mortgage

living paycheck to paycheck

Trillions of Dollars

100

50

0

1990   2000   2010   2020

Wealth for half of America's households has barely budged since 1989. Meanwhile, wealth for the top 1 percent has grown astronomically.

Okay, so who cares about inequality if capitalism let us afford smart-phones and clothes and stuff?

Some capitalists and those who sympathize with them may argue that inequality like this is overstated. I mean, none of us want to go back to transatlantic slavery just because there was more income and wealth equality—or at least I, a Black person, do not want that. And more parity among different income and wealth brackets doesn't necessarily mean people's lives are better.

But that argument is silly, and it's self-serving. I'm sure you've heard some bootlick—I mean very fine people who seem to think they'll be the next Bill Gates say that Americans are better off than people in developing countries because more of us have smartphones! And flat-screen TVs!

Sure, let's praise capitalists for selling us gadgets—clearly they're doing it out of the goodness of their hearts!—but the point isn't that things could be worse. It's how much *better* our lives could be without this kind of system. As another socialist, Nathan J. Robinson, has argued in a really great essay, "You don't measure against what is or what has been, you measure against what could be."

This is especially true for things that really count, like affordable healthcare, housing, and the peace of mind of knowing that you don't have to slave away at two or three jobs or take on mounds of student loan debt just for the chance of a nice quality of life.

We shouldn't allow the capitalistic narrative that things are better off than the past or better than in developing countries— which their own practices of imperialism and colonialism have been largely responsible for under-developing—to dictate what our possibilities are.

You know when you write walls of text to explain something to your significant other, and then they ignore all the valid things you bring up and dispute one little piece of your text? That's what it's like talking to capitalists. On top of wanting life to be better

for most people, finding alternatives to capitalism is important because inequality is just wrong. So there's that.

But lastly, it's important to remember that the unequal prosperity enjoyed by the world's top income earners isn't happening in a vacuum. Often, they're accumulating that wealth on the backs of real people whose very lives are being sacrificed so they can buy a second or third yacht, and the baby yacht that goes into that yacht. Or, y'know, they're sacrificing actual children.

capitali$m has *always* been bad for workers. how bad? *child-slavery* bad.

In England in the 1700s, machinery and the modern factory system had replaced land and rural agriculture as the primary sources of wealth. There was industrial production before this period, but advances in technology facilitated the growth of England's manufacturing cities and subsequently the rise of capitalism.

These advances also created a demand for labor, and men, women, and children were all drawn in to work in factories. This created a new class of industrialists who owned the factories and wanted a class of low-wage laborers—the lower the wages, the more profits for the owners. As technology advanced rapidly, demand for skilled labor went down. With more workers vying for jobs, wages fell. And working conditions declined along with it.

As George Moses Price, a commissioner on the New York State Factory Investigation Commission, described industrialization in Europe:

The worker was drawn away from his peaceful cottage of the agricultural district, with his alternating work at the loom and in the fields, and was transplanted into the poisoned and foul air of the mill, with its whizzing machinery and maddening speed, which petrified his soul, and atrophied the organs of his body, and shortened his days by the cruel haste of the machinery.

And it got worse. With the pool of adult workers getting tapped out, capitalists decided to dip into the kiddie labor pool and recruit children to work for them. When it was hard to find children to work voluntarily, manufacturers bought and trafficked in kids to force them into factories "in a form not different from the methods of ancient and modern slave dealers."

"Direct slavery is as much the pivot of our industrialism today as machinery, credit, etc. Without slavery no cotton; without cotton no modern industry. Slavery has given value to the colonies; the colonies have created world trade; world trade is the necessary condition of large-scale machine industry. . . . Slavery is therefore an economic category of the highest importance."

— Karl Marx, *The Poverty of Philosophy*, 1847

Among these children "there was often no discrimination of sex, and disease, misery, and vice grew as in a hotbed of contagion. Those who tried to run away had irons riveted to their ankles with long links reaching up to the hips and were compelled to work and sleep in these chains. Many died and were buried secretly at night and many committed suicide," Price noted. But capitalism and freedom, right?!

Granted, capitalism has shifted away from some of its worst excesses, thanks to labor movements and public policies that forced it to evolve, including child labor laws, shorter work days, having weekends, and other reforms. But the principles of major companies are still generally the same: Make as much money as you can from other people's labor, and if workers can barely afford rent and other necessities to live comfortably, who cares?

And those conditions were just in the context of an economy built on heavy industry and wage labor.

In the Americas we had our own horrendous system of plantation slavery, which fueled capitalist economies in both northern US cities and in Europe, which we'll get into in Chapter 2. The class of plantation owners who exploited enslaved Black labor weren't industrialists, they didn't provide wages, and the unique challenges of city life and urban squalor—where European capitalists began to concentrate work—were not yet present in the American South. But this reliance on human misery to fuel wealth for an elite few was in full force on both sides of the Atlantic, like with generations of capitalists who followed.

Just think of these guys (because they've mostly, but not exclusively, been dudes) as the most obnoxious contestants on any reality dating show.

John, 28

OCCUPATION: Planter

HOBBIES: Living in a big house and just some lighthearted slave roleplaying to keep my property—I mean love interests—in line

John Jr., 34

OCCUPATION: Factory owner

DISLIKES: Paying people a living wage

LIKES: Threatening to move abroad because you're too demanding and I have prospects all over the world who would be happy with the bare minimum [wage] I bring to the table.

John III, 42

OCCUPATION: Private equity-fund managing partner

WEAKNESS: Investing a little time in a lot of people but not really valuing any of them. I'm just here for a good time, not a long time tbh.

Jeighson, 25

OCCUPATION: Social-media startup founder

WHAT I LOVE ABOUT MY JOB: Secretly collecting all your information and cute little details about you in order to sell you stuff you don't need. I promise I'm a normal human who is not stalking you.

are you
bad and bougie,
or bad and bourgeoisie?

So where do you fit into all of this right now? And why does it matter?

CLASS DISTINCTIONS 101

Once upon a time, two guys from Germany saw the world was shaping up with grotesque inequality between the classes. They also envisioned workers would eventually get fed up and start a revolution to overthrow capitalism. These two guys—Karl Marx and Friedrich Engels—published *The Communist Manifesto* in 1848 (and today you can see twenty-something dudes with mustaches reading it on public transportation all over the world). But their descriptions of different groups of people under capitalism are still used today. Here are the basics:

PROLETARIAT: The working class. They form the majority of the population and work for wages. They do not own what they produce.

PETTY BOURGEOISIE: They fluctuate between the working class and the bourgeoisie. Marx and Engels predicted they would disappear, because capitalists would force them into the working class. Some aspire to be capitalists; others align with the working class.

BOURGEOISIE: The capitalists. They hire and exploit the labor of the proletariat, the working class who work for wages. The bourgeoisie own whatever the working class produces as well as the tools, land, and factories that the proletariat uses to produce goods (i.e., the "means of production"). The profit from this labor is concentrated in the hands of just a few capitalists.

People like Marx and Engels, or Mao Tse-tung in China, or the Black Panthers in the United States—all of whom thought capitalism was fundamentally unfair and exploitative—wanted to know who could be allies in creating a new system.

To be clear, there is no bright-line rule about the number of workers you'd need to hire to make you a capitalist (aka a bourgeois) versus being someone in the petty bourgeoisie with a small, family-run business, or what the clear division is between the proletariat and the petty bourgeoisie.

American leftists may joke about which one-percenters would be saved in a class war (and by "American leftists," I mean myself—and for the record, I'd save Beyoncé). But in the last century and a half, this was a practical problem millions of people had to contend with by engaging in armed conflict.

From Algeria to Kenya, to Vietnam and Chile, revolutionaries wanted to know who in the upper and middle classes they could recruit in their fight for independence from European and white American imperialism, capitalism, and colonialism. If you weren't truly aligned with the working class and felt more tied to imperial, elite business interests—especially because you believed you might ascend to a higher class at some point—you could undermine the entire nation's struggle for independence.

If you're shopping for vegan desserts in Whole Foods, but you're not the type of person who'd pay your workers as little as possible so you can afford to fly off into space, you might be "bougie" but you're probably not Elon Musk–level corporate mob boss. Being a consumer doesn't make you a capitalist.

But even if you are bougie and can afford nice (perhaps gluten-free) things, a look at the writings of really smart people who have critiqued capitalism shows that your status among the "petty bourgeoisie," or middle class, isn't necessarily fixed. You can technically be better off than the proletariat at one point in time but be one or two unfortunate circumstances—a bad year in sales, a medical emergency, or a home foreclosure—away from a challenging economic position. Capitalists don't live in this kind of precarity; they help create it for others.

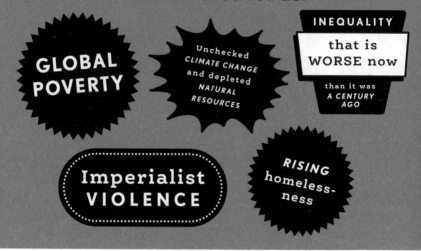

This is the world capitali$m has created for us:

GLOBAL POVERTY

Unchecked CLIMATE CHANGE and depleted NATURAL RESOURCES

INEQUALITY

that is WORSE now

than it was A CENTURY AGO

Imperialist VIOLENCE

RISING homeless-ness

Another way to think about it is this: How invested are you in capitalism? Basically, if there was a chance that another system, like socialism, was on the horizon, would you align with workers fighting for equality, or would you resist change because you're committed to maintaining and accumulating more wealth and status within the old system? Do you want to become the toxic bae one day, or are you working toward a relationship where you and your partner—and everyone—can prosper?

If you struggle to see where you fit in here, or have apprehensions about losing the little stability you might have already worked so hard for, it's understandable. The propaganda machine that treats capitalism like the prince in shining armor rescuing us from scary commie lefties stealing our freedom has been operating in full force all our lives. Maybe, *maybe*, it's time for a change. Looking at how capitalism has been built directly by creating and maintaining racial hierarchies reveals just one more reason to leave capitalism behind. 👊

The Boy Is (Not) Mine

"CAPITALISM WANTS TO DIVIDE US TO
DOMINATE US AND DOMINATE US TO ROB US."
—EVO MORALES

Imagine being in a relationship with someone for years only to discover they had a whole secret life on racist message boards railing about white people getting replaced by people of color. You go through their search history and stuff like "January 6 meetups" pops up all over the results. It's like you never even knew this person. And they have a Black best friend and everything; how could they possibly be a racist neo-Nazi nutcase? Capitalism has been living this double life. It props up POC friends on commercials and billboards. Big corporations tweet out solidarity statements and roll out the ethnic-themed products for every holiday possible. Meanwhile, capitalists have used race to create an underclass of workers and to throw a wrench into working-class solidarity for generations. It's not that they just love chaos. They love to profit and play us against our supposed differences, even if it leads to violence and animosity.

You think you know two-faced creeps from Tinder? Or that dude Brandy & Monica were fighting over in "That Boy Is Mine"? Well, meet American capitalists. The United States is a prime example of just how effective a player capitalism has been.

w. e. b. du bois shows us the receipts

Marx and Engels have influenced generations of leaders across the globe who have fought for independence from the dominant capitalist class. But scholars outside of Europe also realized the OG communist theories weren't one-size-fits-all, especially given how integral racism was in creating and maintaining capitalism in other parts of the world. Things got especially messy when you tried to apply their solutions to America.

The racism these scholars were talking about wasn't merely the kind that fuels your Uncle Larry on his rants about "the" Blacks and Mexicans at the Thanksgiving table. They were referring to laws and practices that have treated masses of people—Black people in particular—as too inferior to even be regarded as citizens and members of society, let alone part of the working class.

While racism in and of itself deserves attention, they knew that racism was interwoven with class antagonism.

Remember that friend with the Google-stalking skills who finds all the dirt on your latest crush, like, instantly and unsolicited? That's W. E. B. Du Bois for capitalism. If you need to choose your fighter in the class war—and someone who fundamentally understands the challenges of racism in that war—he's definitely a good one to start with, although we'll meet more Class Warriors throughout the coming chapters.

Du Bois thought Marx and Engels had the right diagnosis for capitalism in Europe, but he showed that their analysis couldn't be perfectly applied to the United States. He argued that it wasn't only white capitalists who harmed Black workers by treating them as property and forcing them to toil on their land. The white *proletariat* harmed Black people, too.

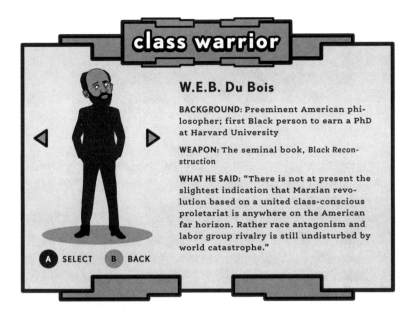

class warrior

W.E.B. Du Bois

BACKGROUND: Preeminent American philosopher; first Black person to earn a PhD at Harvard University

WEAPON: The seminal book, Black Reconstruction

WHAT HE SAID: "There is not at present the slightest indication that Marxian revolution based on a united class-conscious proletariat is anywhere on the American far horizon. Rather race antagonism and labor group rivalry is still undisturbed by world catastrophe."

A SELECT   B BACK

While some Black people were steadily escaping to freedom by moving north and the abolition movement was at a peak, millions of the European workers that Marx and Engels were working to radicalize were also moving to northern cities in America. Instead of sticking around to overthrow capitalism (or feudalism, in places where industrialization had not yet taken hold) back home in Europe, much of the white proletariat simply migrated to get the better wages handed down from a different set of elites in the US.

This group of migrants didn't necessarily align with Black workers, who might otherwise have been their natural allies in northern factory cities like Boston, New York, and Philadelphia. On the contrary, some European workers were intent on maligning them, sometimes violently. The 1863 New York City race massacre was a prime example.

The 1863 New York City race massacre

At the beginning of the Civil War, Black people weren't considered citizens and were technically ineligible to be drafted in war (though they served through other means). White working-class immigrants, however, could be drafted.

In New York, pro-slavery Democratic Party leaders warned that emancipation and the "nigger war" would lead to a flood of southern Blacks competing with white workers. As historian Leslie Harris notes, "in the midst of wartime economic distress, [the white working class] believed that their political leverage and economic status was rapidly declining as blacks appeared to be gaining power."

To protest the draft, in July 1863 largely Irish immigrants in New York City attacked government buildings in what has become known as the Civil War Draft Riots. They then moved on to a Black orphanage, setting it on fire, before targeting symbols of Black mobility. The 233 children who were in the orphanage escaped and were spared, but other Black New Yorkers were not, including Black men who were subjected to torture, lynching, and murder across five days of mob violence. With this fierce public terror, including eleven lynchings of Black men, the riots forced hundreds of Black people out of New York City.

An article from the *New-York Tribune* on July 14, 1863, paints a haunting picture:

> As if by preconcerted action an attack was made upon colored men and boys in every part of the city during the day. . . . A small colored boy, about 9 years old, was set upon and hunted at the corner of Broadway and Chambers street by the mob. He jumped on a two-horse wagon that was passing by, when stones and sticks were hurled at him from every quarter. . . . The Orphan Asylum was fired about 5 o'clock in the afternoon. The infuriated mob, eager for any outrage, were turned that way by the simple suggestion that the building was full of colored children. They clamored around the house like demons, filling the air with yells.

Sooo you can see, it was one thing to theorize about a unified working class. Putting the revolution into practice was another story.

And it wasn't just everyday white workers—or European immigrants who were in the process of becoming "white" Americans—who harmed Black workers. White labor leaders' attitudes toward Black workers and abolition ranged from apathetic to hostile.

Engels published a handy Q&A about communism in 1847, before he cowrote *The Communist Manifesto* with Marx. In it, he suggested that communists build international alliances, but as Du Bois laid out in *Black Reconstruction in America, 1860–1880* (seriously, Du Bois had all the tea), Engels hardly mentioned slavery, glaringly omitting the potential allyship of four million workers, the estimated Black US population around that time. To be clear, Marx was a staunch advocate of abolition precisely because he saw it as a blow to capitalism. But white American labor leaders and the white left in Europe's capitalist countries often didn't follow suit.

In other cases, white Northerners explicitly prioritized white workers over enslaved Blacks. Horace Greeley—the New-York Tribune publisher who hired Karl Marx and put him on the map in American media—even said: "if I am less troubled concerning the slavery prevalent in Charleston or New Orleans, it is because I see so much slavery in New York which appears to claim my first efforts," by which he meant, ahem, white people.

Some white labor leaders, like Hermann Kriege, even refused to support abolition because he thought it could make the conditions of his "white brothers" "infinitely worse."

"The history of all hitherto existing society is the history of class struggles." —*The Communist Manifesto*

This was Marx and Engels's call to action to bring the proletariat together to wrest power from the ownership class and distribute that power to workers. But with millions of members of the Black proletariat effectively excluded from the Northern industrial working-class and labor movements by its leaders and media, how many troops could actually be rallied to end capitalism?

Um, looking at where we are today: not enough.

being white is the new asset

Beyond showing how the white American labor movement deliberately excluded Black workers, Du Bois highlighted something else important about the intersection of race and class: whiteness had become its own material interest.

Race isn't merely a color or a phenotype, but an asset. In the US, being white has made it easier to buy land (or receive it for free!!) and expand west, as provided by the Homestead Act of 1863. It has meant having higher wages in public-sector jobs, as Jim Crow era laws mandated. It has meant qualifying for federally backed home loans in the New Deal. Today, it means living in neighborhoods that—all else being equal—have higher home values merely because white people live there, amounting to $156 billion in cumulative losses for Black households. It means

inheriting wealth from the previous generation's homes and assets that were acquired in part thanks to those earlier racist policies, and that continue to appreciate today. And so white wealth continues to accumulate and far outpace Black wealth, and this shows no signs of stopping.

To recap, racism—and specifically anti-Black racism—in the Industrial Revolution kept a unified working class from forming just as capitalism was becoming dominant in America. Still, Du Bois didn't seem to argue that a united proletariat could exist in America in the future; he was just describing things as they were.

Remember in the iconic "The Boy Is Mine" video when Brandy and Monica finally decided to stop singing at each other through the wall (why were the walls that thin??) and confront their two-timing boyfriend?? Yeah, we need to do that.

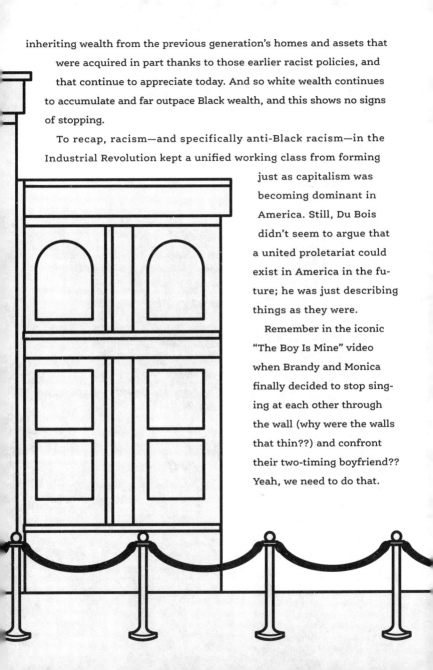

A Rare Case of Racial Solidarity

AS YOU'VE READ, northern white labor organizers were often reluctant to bring Black people into the fold of the labor movement, and some were downright racist. This in turn made a lot of Black workers skeptical about unionizing in the early 1900s. But in Chicago in the 1930s, a variety of forces allowed some workers of Chicago's meatpacking companies to align together in a union and push back against the big bosses of the industry.

At the time, the big labor groups, the American Federation of Labor and Congress of Industrial Organizations, had recently split up. The former was seen as hostile to Black people, but the CIO, a coalition of various unions, was influenced by left and communist organizers who stressed racial equality.   The Packinghouse Workers' Organizing Committee (PWOC), a group within the CIO, actively fought against racial discrimination in Chicago.

This explicit commitment to racial justice in Chicago won the trust of Black workers, who were often relegated to stockyards and had no opportunity for career advancement. The lack of upward mobility got worse during the Great Depression, as companies were quicker to fire Black people. This made the city's Black meatpackers less trusting of their employers, and they became some of the most militant union members, a complete shift from just a decade prior.

As writer Paul Street noted, "[B]lacks in the stockyards would not have overcome their tendency to side with capital over labor without the formation of a union remarkable for the depth of its commitment to addressing black workers' special concerns."

This included criticizing "the packers' 'lily white' job ceiling, threaten[ing] to expel white union members who voice racist sentiments," and instituting an early form of affirmative action—they won an agreement with one meatpacking company to hire Black workers based on their proportion to Chicago's population.

Street recounts a passage from the Chicago Defender, the city's Black paper and staunch critic of the city's racist unions, which stated that:

because the PWOC planted the seed of unity . . . Negroes walk freely and in safety. Any public place which refused them service would be quickly put out of business by a boycott of the white union members. On the very streets where danger once lurked for Negroes, colored men stop for long chats about baseball with Polish or Irish workers.

If the Chicago meatpackers are any model for us today, it shows that even in one of the country's most segregated cities, at a time when anti-Blackness was more entrenched than it is now, making an express commitment to antiracism didn't necessarily put off white workers. Having a culture of unity, like PWOC did, genuine interracial alliances, and a shared class identity is always nice. Or at the very least, the union's willingness to kick out racist members was enough of an incentive for white workers to stick with the union, lest they also part with the higher quality of life they were granted by being in it. Nothing like a little shame to get people to do the right thing! The kids may call this cancel culture, but the CIO found it to be a successful organizing tool.

the first n-word— no, not that one

Essentially since they arrived, Europeans relied on indigenous Americans, Africans, and white indentured servants to toil on land in the New World, but they eventually began to shift more to African labor. Their overreliance on Africans led to Western Europeans and settlers in the Americas creating an explicitly anti-Black racial hierarchy to maintain this vital source of labor. So yes, it was about money.

Enter the creation of the first N-word: the Negro. Europeans invented the term *Negro* as a catchall for Africans of various ethnic groups. This wasn't merely an "idle exercise in racial and moral schemata," scholar Cedric J. Robinson pointed out. Its specific purpose was to expand capitalism. This "fiction of a dumb beast of burden fit only for slavery . . .

Blacks came to signify a difference of species, an exploitable source of energy (labor power) both mindless to the organizational requirements of production and insensitive to the subhuman conditions of work.

– Cedric J. Robinson

MAKING UP WORDS
=
MAKING MONEY

was closely associated with the economic, technical, and financial requirements of Western development from the sixteenth century on." No
longer were enslaved Africans Ibo, Yoruba, Mandingo, Fulani, Hausa, or
the other myriad ethnicities from the west coast of Africa, where most
enslaved people were captured. Those forced into the Transatlantic Slave
Trade were lumped into a singular subhuman category and ripped of
their historical contributions.

Anti-Black racism became especially pernicious and widespread as
abolition threatened to end this seemingly limitless source of enslaved
Black labor, with the American government at every level espousing
anti-Black myths to maintain its economic growth. This racism continued
in America through the late nineteenth and twentieth centuries, as
emancipated African Americans and Black migrants began to compete
with white labor.

Europeans from a wide variety of disciplines got in on the anti-Black
slander to fuel the engines of capitalism and colonialism, including some
major heroes of European and American history. Even though they knew
Africans weren't that different from them, they invented an assortment
of negative qualities to further their power and wealth . . . kinda like those
people who neg you into dating them. Except the negging got us enslaved
instead of just stuck on a bad date. Negging. Negro. Coincidence? I think
not! (Actually, it definitely is.)

NEGGING

Super cool, totally not racist quotes from

"Their round eyes, squat noses, and invariable thick lips, the different configuration of their ears, their woolly heads, and the measure of their intellects, make a prodigious difference between them and other species of men."

Francois-Marie Voltaire, 1765

"The Negro, who is well suited to his climate, namely strong, fleshy, and agile. However because he is so amply supplied by his motherland, he is also lazy, indolent, and dawdling."

Arthur de Gobineau, 1853

"Thus, the European nations, owing to the brilliance of their scientific knowledge and the clear outlines of their civilization, are obviously in the full glare of day, while the negroes sleep in the darkness of ignorance, and the Chinese live in a half-light that gives them an incomplete, though powerful, social development. As for the Redskins, who are gradually disappearing from the earth, where can we find a more beautiful image of their fate than the setting sun?"

Immanuel Kant, 1777

THE NEGRO

famous European and American philosophers

"I advance it therefore as a suspicion only, that the blacks, whether originally a distinct race, or made distinct by time and circumstances, are inferior to the whites in the endowments both of body and mind. It is not against experience to suppose, that different species of the same genus, or varieties of the same species, may possess different qualifications . . . This unfortunate difference of color, and perhaps of faculty, is a powerful obstacle to the emancipation of these people."

Thomas
··· Jefferson,
1781

"Negroes are to be regarded as a race of children who remain immersed in their state of uninterested naïveté. They are sold, and let themselves be sold, without any reflection on the rights or wrongs of the matter."

"The Negro represents natural man in all his wild and untamed nature. If you want to treat and understand him rightly, you must abstract all elements of respect and morality and sensitivity—there is nothing remotely humanized in the Negro character."

Georg ···
Hegel,
1817

This anti-Black shift devolved into an entire ideology of white supremacy that resulted in grotesque and inhumane laws and customs such as the Jim Crow laws of the twentieth century.

These were also intended to limit worker organizing or any possible rebellion across race lines.

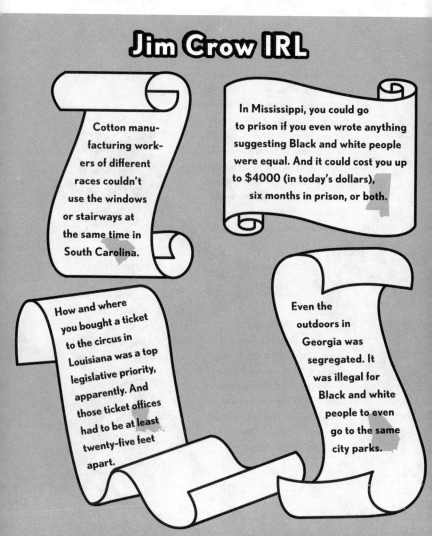

Jim Crow IRL

Cotton manufacturing workers of different races couldn't use the windows or stairways at the same time in South Carolina.

In Mississippi, you could go to prison if you even wrote anything suggesting Black and white people were equal. And it could cost you up to $4000 (in today's dollars), six months in prison, or both.

How and where you bought a ticket to the circus in Louisiana was a top legislative priority, apparently. And those ticket offices had to be at least twenty-five feet apart.

Even the outdoors in Georgia was segregated. It was illegal for Black and white people to even go to the same city parks.

colonizers, the original scammers

Extracting cheap labor from a bunch of people and arbitrarily dividing them based on their appearance weren't the only practices that helped build capitalism. Colonizing the New World—and then colonizing countries outside of the Americas—provided one of the main streams of capital for Western Europe's industrialization.

As Great Britain, Belgium, and France shifted to industrial economies, they needed more natural resources to meet their increased capacity. So they had the brilliant idea to just occupy other places—Africa and Asia—to meet that need.

Industrialists compelled workers in African and Asian countries to extract natural resources cheaply (and for much lower wages than European workers would tolerate). These raw materials were then used to manufacture goods in factories that capitalists owned in Europe and other places.

Sometimes the finished products would be exported back to the same Asian and African workers who extracted them (at high costs, obviously), ensuring that industrial European countries continued to profit from Africa and Asia at every stage of production. This is the essence of colonialism, and it was an absolute racket.

"The colonies have become the dumping ground, and colonial peoples the false recipients, of manufactured goods of the industrialists and capitalists of Great Britain, France, Belgium and other colonial powers who turn to the dependent territories which feed their industrial plants. This is colonialism in a nutshell."

– **Kwame Nkrumah,**
*Towards Colonial
Freedom,* circa 1942

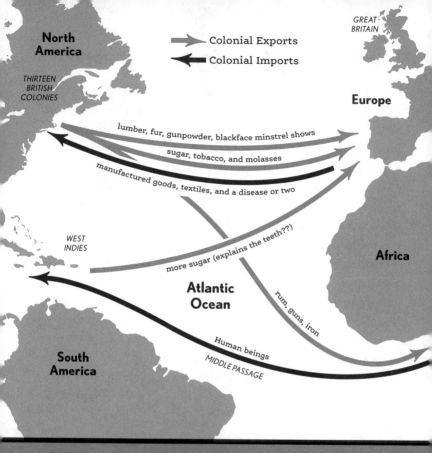

North America

THIRTEEN BRITISH COLONIES

GREAT BRITAIN

Europe

Colonial Exports
Colonial Imports

lumber, fur, gunpowder, blackface minstrel shows

sugar, tobacco, and molasses

manufactured goods, textiles, and a disease or two

WEST INDIES

more sugar (explains the teeth??)

Atlantic Ocean

Africa

rum, guns, iron

South America

Human beings
MIDDLE PASSAGE

REAL GREAT TRADEOFFS HERE!
For the small cost of enslaving entire humans, rich white people got to have more sugar.

Africa bore the brunt of this colonial capitalism. During the transatlantic slave trade, European contact with Africa was mostly limited to trading posts along the coasts. But explorers began to navigate the continent's interior in the late 1800s, leading European leaders to realize there was money to be made on the continent, kickstarting the "Scramble for Africa" and leading to the Berlin Conference that divvied up the continent.

Before the conference, only 10 percent of Africa was colonized by Europeans. By the end of it, Europeans had made plans to colonize 90 percent of it.

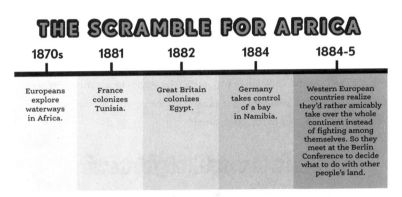

THE SCRAMBLE FOR AFRICA

1870s	1881	1882	1884	1884-5
Europeans explore waterways in Africa.	France colonizes Tunisia.	Great Britain colonizes Egypt.	Germany takes control of a bay in Namibia.	Western European countries realize they'd rather amicably take over the whole continent instead of fighting among themselves. So they meet at the Berlin Conference to decide what to do with other people's land.

And can we just pause here. Because it wasn't enough that Spain and Great Britain enriched themselves by colonizing the Americas and amassing wealth through sugar and textile production. It wasn't enough that, for centuries, Europeans were already becoming wealthy by trading with Asia and Africa. It wasn't enough that they profited from others' land and labor. Greed propelled these colonial capitalists to earn "superprofits," paying even lower wages to the people of color they colonized than to the workers in their home countries.

And this isn't a fluke in the system, and the system surely isn't a relic of the past. You see it today in our class structures and even in our love lives. Some people enter relationships and just want to benefit as much as possible, even if their partner is left high and dry, doing all the emotional labor and somehow feeling guilty or confused when nothing changes, when it's still not enough for the jerk.

Today, capitalism compels the ownership class to continually amass more capital with less input and cheaper labor in order to remain competitive, just as the colonial powers of the past competed internationally for resources and workers to plunder. So what if it meant millions of people would come to be considered an inferior race, with lasting, *devastating* effects for a few centuries?

It's hard to be surprised that the anti-Black racism Europeans and American settlers used to justify slavery in the 1700s spawned anti-Black racism for hundreds of years afterward. It's also not surprising this racism led colonial capitalists to justify why Africans on the continent deserved drastically lower wages than their European counterparts. It just kept working for them. No brainer!

what's it worth right now?

So what's the point of all this? Why does it matter how capitalism started? Maybe it has finally changed (despite leaving a trail of heartbroken victims along the way)!

For one, history shows that we've never seen a capitalist system free of exploitation, whether it's enslaving Africans; colonizing African, Asian, or indigenous American territories to take their natural resources; exploiting the labor of wage workers; or inventing racist myths to justify their practices and create divisions among the working class. So-called "late capitalism" isn't some recent, dystopian reality. The system was built this way, from Day One.

The high standard of living that Europe's capitalist countries began to enjoy didn't arrive magically at their doorsteps. It was possible because of the exploitation of their colonies. And some activists, scholars, and economists like to focus on capitalist social democratic countries like Sweden or Norway as contemporary models for socialism. But this

ignores their historic (and continued!!) exploitation of non-European countries that enables their current high standard of living. As W. E. B. Du Bois said: "the laboring class in western Europe and America was being bribed by high wages that came not so much out of the profits of the employers as out of the low wages of colored labor."

Capitalism won't save us because that defies its fundamental logic. The goal of capitalism is to maximize profit, so there will always be a race to the bottom for wages—with a little hush money thrown our way sometimes (stock options! healthcare!) so we don't revolt—but these are whispered sweet nothings. We'll get into why in the next chapters.

Europe and the US are still using the cheap labor of the Global South today, occupying foreign countries, getting into wars to extract natural resources, and intervening in foreign governments to expand capitalist markets.

> "The United States and its junior European partners are pursuing the same old policies with new means. The old colonial policies had left the colonized societies exploited, penetrated, and fragmented. The new form of empire building now masquerades under the most sophisticated brand of imperialist thinking—globalization!"
>
> **– Kema Irogbe,** *The Effects of Globalization in Latin America, Africa, and Asia*

why can't rainbow capitalism save us?

Some may argue that the system itself is fine, we just need more compassionate capitalists. Or people say we need to simply diversify the ranks of the capitalists in power. Throw some more women and people of color in boardrooms and give communities of color capital so they, too, can be capitalists. That sounds nice, right?

But some scholars say that the fundamental nature of capitalism wouldn't even allow capitalism to be truly diverse. Economist Abram Harris presented that argument in his work "The Negro As Capitalist" in 1936, where he wrote:

> As long as capitalism remains, it is reasonably certain that the main arteries of commerce, industry, credit and finance will be controlled by white capitalists. Under the circumstances, the great mass of black and white men will continue dependent upon these capitalists for their livelihood, and the small Negro business man and the small white capitalist will continue to subordinate to these larger finance and industrial interests.

Almost 90 years later, Harris' predictions remain true. Despite all the exposure given to rich Black celebrities and athletes, just one Black person, Nigerian cement manufacturer Aliko Dagnote, appeared in the top 400 of Forbes' world's richest people in 2021. One!!

And although Black Americans romanticize Tulsa's "Black Wall Street" and other centers of Black entrepreneurship that were separate from white communities in the 20th century, studies show entrepreneurship generally just expands the wealth gap because it's most accessible to people who are already pretty well-off. Instead of lifting the average American into higher class ranks, it mostly lifts up those who already have access and resources.

$100,000

The net worth of those most likely to undertake self-employment in 1995, before becoming self-employed

25 years later

$380,000

Net worth of average self-employed family in 2019

$24,100

Median Black household net worth in 2019, still just a quarter of what was likely required to start a business over TWO DECADES ago

Without the starting point of having a ton of money to begin with, most people aren't going to magically small-business their way into wealth and financial freedom. As Harris argued, "the independent black economy, whether it develops upon the basis of private profit or of cooperation, cannot be the means of achieving the Negro's economic salvation."

And even if the majority of Black people somehow happened upon piles of money and all decided to own a small business, and they all hired Black workers (practically a fantasy unless the federal government somehow gets a conscience and pays trillions of dollars in reparations), Marxists would say that changing the face of the petty bourgeoisie doesn't change the fundamentally exploitative nature of the owner-worker relationship.

We've had 300 years of capitalism now, so why hasn't the compassion dominated it yet? Why has the racial wealth gap only gotten larger, even worse than it was in the late 1960s at the tail end of the Jim Crow era? How much longer should we give capitalism a shot? Twenty years? Fifty? One hundred?

In the meantime, we have a dying planet, constant wars, mass hunger, poverty, and inequality, while the people who created and uphold these conditions continue to be enriched.

Capitalism basically created interracial animosity and now gets to be the dude with baddie R&B singers fighting with each other instead of challenging him, while he sits back and enjoys the drama.

So, are we going to dump that MFer already? ✊🏾

3
Art Freaks

"THERE WAS NOT A SINGLE LIBERATION MOVEMENT
IN AFRICA THAT WAS NOT FIGHTING FOR SOCIALISM."
—ASSATA SHAKUR

I know, I know. Easier said than done. You and your other half seemed like such a perfect match. You both like that random band that hardly anyone else knows about, and something about her Capricorn moon aligning with your Leo sun told you this was meant to be. But next thing you know, this intoxicating love interest has started telling you to hang out with your friends less. Those people aren't good for you—they're not even real friends—you start to realize under the influence of the romance. So you start mostly hanging out with your beau, who gets you. You notice little jealous tendencies, perhaps *vaguely* controlling behaviors, but that's just love, isn't it? Who else out there would care for you so much, love you so deeply, that they would act totally nuts and make up lies about people when they sense you might be giving literally anyone else the time of day??

This is how capitalism treats us. We've been convinced that our current system is the natural order of things based on pseudoscience about human behavior and the supposed fact that nothing else works. There's no better option! Anything else will actually be more harmful to us, we're told, no matter what abuses we endure under capitalism. And if it leaves some people in the dust, you can't worry about that, right? Just stay in your own little bubble, follow the rules, and you'll be okay.

We live in a world where money and resources are hoarded by a wealthy few. Yet we're told that it's under socialism that hard-working people will have their money seized to benefit lazy strangers. If there is one thing that amuses me most about capitalist propaganda, it is its ability to convince people that what we see capitalism doing isn't actually what we see it doing.

While a few multinational companies control the media we consume, the music we listen to, and the food we eat, it's socialism that supposedly lacks choice and freedom. It's definitely giving the Plastics from Mean Girls, and capitalism is the Queen B!$$#.

Regina's got Aaron Samuels—and practically everyone else, even the principal!—all wrapped up in her status and false promises. Meanwhile, the art freaks are super aware of the madness playing out, and they try to give you the intel, to show you there's a way out of there, but they're just treated like outcasts.

We hear so much about what socialism is through the myths purported by the rich Regina Georges of the world. This chapter is dedicated to uncovering how socialism really works, challenging the myths we might not even realize we've bought into. And yes, we need a whole chapter to do this, because leftists like to disagree on things and there's not a simple answer.

this could be us, but we're tripping over capitalism

We've been so busy chasing capitalism's heart for, you know, the entire history of America, that we haven't spent time getting know socialism. Socialism as a buzzword has become more popular and appealing in the last few years, but what is it, really?

The truth is, you'll hear somewhat different definitions of *socialism* from different people. Throughout its history, there hasn't been a consensus of what exactly it entails, and even Marx and Engels didn't get into a lot of detail about what it should look like in practice.

Essentially, socialism means that workers own the means of production in society—including the factories, natural resources, technology, machinery, and other things necessary to produce our goods and services—and workers democratically decide how the profit from their own labor is distributed and how companies and organizations are run.

This contrasts with capitalism, as we know, where a much smaller ownership class (the bourgeoisie) primarily owns the means of production and the goods their workers produce, and a relatively small board of directors in these companies decide how profits are spent.

Black Panther Party leader Assata Shakur put it simply:

"[A]nything that has any kind of value is made, mined, grown, produced, and processed by working people. So why shouldn't working people collectively own that wealth? Why shouldn't working people own and control their own resources? Capitalism meant that rich businessmen owned the wealth, while socialism meant that the people who made the wealth owned it."

– Assata Shakur

Another way of thinking about socialism is that it's an experiment in workplace democracy, where everyday people have primary control over how their jobs—the places where they spend most of their lives—are run.

While conservatives and so-called moderates on both sides of the aisle paint socialism as a scary, radical alternative, even as fundamentally un-American, ideas from socialists have long been a part of mainstream American politics, more than we realize.

In one state, socialists and other leftists were the driving force behind America's earliest investments in public infrastructure, popular progressive policies, and social programs that we still have today. And no, it wasn't one of those "coastal elite" states that Republicans insist is poisoning the minds of children with, you know, books. In fact, this was all going down in their favorite region—America's Heartland®.

wisconsin, land of the free

Before it was known for the Green Bay Packers, cheese, and a random T-Pain shout-out just so he could rhyme something with "mansion," Wisconsin was home to the first and only socialist mayors of any major US city. This wasn't by accident.

From academic to legislative halls, socialists and labor leaders exerted political influence throughout Wisconsin in the early 1900s. Their work became models for other states across the country and eventually impacted federal social policy.

A major figure in Wisconsin's progressivism of the time was socialist economist John R. Commons. While the prominent "Chicago School" of economics, just one state south in Illinois, endorsed laissez-faire capitalism free of government intervention, Commons led the "Wisconsin School" that valued workers.

"Wisconsin School" economists wanted to eliminate unemployment, help workers secure competitive wages, and enact child labor laws. They also advocated for workplace democracy, where workers have more decision-making power at their jobs.

These ideas eventually inspired federal action, too. As writer Dan Kaufman notes, "The New Deal demonstrated the Wisconsin Idea on a national scale, introducing the first real social welfare system in the United States."

STARTED IN WISCONSIN ... NOW WE'RE HERE

First state with unemployment insurance Each of the 50 states now administer unemployment insurance programs.

First state with a workers' compensation law Every state (plus DC) has laws regulating workers' compensation.

First state to recognize the right to collective bargaining for public employees
- Nearly 34% of public-sector workers are union members.
- That's 5 times higher than private sector workers across the country.
- States with mandatory collective bargaining laws increase the wages of public sector workers by 6 percent.

Wisconsin progressives like Wilbur Cohen and Arthur Alatmeyer served on a federal New Deal Committee Cohen designed Medicare; Alatmeyer became the commissioner for social security, leading a committee to draft the Social Security Act.

For socialists in Wisconsin, 1910 was a year like no other:

- Its most populous city, Milwaukee, gave America its first socialist mayor, Emil Seidel, who kinda got radicalized through woodcarving.

- More socialists were elected to the city council and county board than either Democrats or Republicans.

- Fourteen socialists were elected to the state legislature.

- They sent the first socialist to Congress, Victor Berger, who served in the House of Representatives for four terms.

While some self-proclaimed Wisconsin socialists, like Commons, sought to regulate and save capitalism by making it better for workers, others favored a full transition to state and municipal ownership of industry and the replacement of capitalism altogether.

To be clear, many socialists at the time (and today; seriously the argument is over a century old) argue that state ownership of industry is not socialism. Putting that lengthy debate aside, though, it is generally assumed that moving ownership away from the private capitalist class reduces their power to exploit labor and disadvantage workers.

In Milwaukee in the early 1900s, without a working-class revolution to wrest power and property away from multimillionaire business owners, socialists had to make do with progressive reforms, public infrastructure investments, and modest city ownership of some goods and services.

Under Daniel Hoan, Milwaukee's second and longest-running socialist mayor, who spent twenty-four years in office, the city owned a stone quarry, a street repair shop, and a street lighting distribution center. The Hoan administration also significantly invested in city parks, playgrounds, and social centers, doubling the park system from 960 acres in 1921 to 1,917 acres by 1934.

The socialist reign continued with Frank Zeidler, who served until 1960 as the last socialist mayor of any big American city. And imagine. All of this was in "Real America," not some scary foreign country where right-wingers insist the word choice doesn't exist (i.e., a place where they have good healthcare).

And just a bit further south, like Deep South, a group of Black Americans started a movement to develop their own model of socialism. I grew up in this movement.

ms jackson (not the outkast hit)

The South is known for lots of things. Great food. Warm weather. The Florida Man.

What it's not exactly known for are leftist, socialist politics. But during the Black Power movement, a group of Black people, whose families once migrated out of the South to places like Detroit and Chicago, decided to return to their roots.

The group formed the Republic of New Afrika in 1968, and they made Jackson, Mississippi, their headquarters, where one of their founders was eventually elected mayor in 2013: Chokwe Lumumba, Sr., a revolutionary Black socialist. To summarize about fifty years of history in half a page, it went a little something like this:

After being founded by Imari Obadele, Chokwe Lumumba, Sr., Robbie Williams, and Queen Mother Moore, the RNA establishes the following economic tenets:

People are trained and assigned work in accordance with their preference, their ability and the needs of the Community and the Nation . . .

After community NEEDS are satisfied, wealth is equally divided among all workers . . .

ALL industry and agriculture are owned by the people as a whole and administered by the Republic of New Africa . . .

- Then Lumumba co-founded the Malcolm X Grassroots Movement with other RNA members and started chapters all over the country.
- MXGM organizes around people's assemblies and the Jackson-Kush Plan (we have more on that! Keep reading!), leading to the election of Chokwe Lumumba, Sr. as Jackson's mayor in 2013.

One of the minds behind this ongoing—yes, like right now!—socialist project known as the Jackson-Kush Plan (commonly referred to as the

Jackson Plan) is Kali Akuno. As he wrote in 2017, the Jackson Plan envisions the Southern city with a solidarity economy consisting of "a network of cooperative and mutually reinforcing enterprises and institutions, specifically worker, consumer, and housing cooperatives, and community development credit unions." Under the plan, activists in the movement would also work to build "sustainable, Green (re)development and Green economy networks and enterprises, starting with a Green housing initiative."

Local government would also be seen as a way to provide public finance for community development and "to ensure there is adequate infrastructure to provide quality healthcare, accessible mass transportation, and decent, affordable public housing," among other public necessities. The election of Chokwe Lumumba, Sr. was a huge step in using the public sector to create a more democratic, equitable, and healthy city. Lumumba's untimely death within months of his administration's start slowed that progress, but the seeds have been planted, in seemingly unlikely soil.

So socialists want all kinds of cool things for us, like equality. And also things that capitalists say they want, like freedom and democracy.

But being the jealous, controlling partner that it is, capitalism has convinced us that it's the only system that can provide for us. Like, "I like *invented* her" style. This isn't because we just intrinsically believe

Free the Land

THE LAND
THE BLOOD
THE PEOPLE

Six-year-old Malaika, the New Afrikan Scout

capitalism is the best. We've been played. A heavy, century-long stream of anti-communist and pro-capitalist propaganda and policy from a relatively small group of people actually worked. Who knew? I'm not saying we're brainwashed but . . .

more than mccarthyism

Socialism was never dominant in America, but it wasn't unheard of, either. Socialists gained traction in city and state governments and labor movements particularly in the early 1900s, and not just in Wisconsin. Nearly a million Americans voted for third-party socialist candidate Eugene Debs in the 1912 presidential election (with Wisconsin mayor and socialist Emil Seidel serving as his VP running mate), and the Socialist Party of America was considered one of the largest socialist movements in the world in this era.

As socialism and communism grew to be a steady presence in the US, and Russia became a more dominant political force in the world, capitalist propaganda and anti-communist policy in the US federal government became more prominent, leading to the first Red Scare, from 1917–1920. Even before McCarthyism, which is more famous, America was riling up its red baiting. Just a couple highlights:

1886 Haymarket Affair: (love when history refers to something as an "affair." This one could also be called a "murder."): After a peaceful rally protesting labor conditions in Chicago, a bomb was thrown at police officers, leading to a violent confrontation. US newspapers attributed the violence to socialists and anarchists participating in the strike. Four anarchists were sentenced to death by hanging, even though it wasn't proven that they were involved with the explosion. The final jury was entirely made up of white-collar business workers.

1917 Espionage Act and 1919 Sedition Act: This pair of Congressional laws paid special attention to socialists, and some sections of the Espionage Act were used to prohibit the distribution of leftist newspapers. Under the Sedition Act, those sympathetic to Russia's Bolshevik revolution were prosecuted.

Around this time, the Justice Department conducted systematic raids on communist headquarters. Of course, capitalists got the sense that people were becoming more curious about leaving them behind, and elites had to get more controlling. Go America!

News media has consistently been a messy industry that lives for drama. Press coverage during the first Red Scare aligned with the pro-business agenda of the media owners. Regin Schmidt, in *Red Scare: FBI and the Origins of Anticommunism in the United States*, shows that before McCarthyism went full swing, most of the larger, influential newspapers, including the *New York Times* and the *Washington Post*, "spread right-wing political propaganda."

That's when they weren't dramatizing left-wing activism. Coverage of World War I negotiations wasn't getting the attention that the newspapers expected, so they sensationalized socialist activism for engagement, like content creators on TikTok who exaggerate how chaotic things are for clicks. Nothing new here!

Capitalists talked a lot of crap about their competition (obviously) so that we weren't tempted to get back out there and choose better. Let's look at some of the myths they created that still keep us in a chokehold.

myth 1—socialism is when no freedom

Capitalism has practically become a synonym for America at this point. And America means freedom. So, dusting off those high school logic games, capitalism must mean freedom, too, right? And what's more American than the freedom to choose your own healthcare, where you go to school, the type of food you buy, and, the most coveted freedom of all, to face-mask or not to face-mask! This appeal to "freedom" has governed our discourse for decades.

Just take a look at some public feedback from Americans who invoked communism to decry innocuous federal regulations:

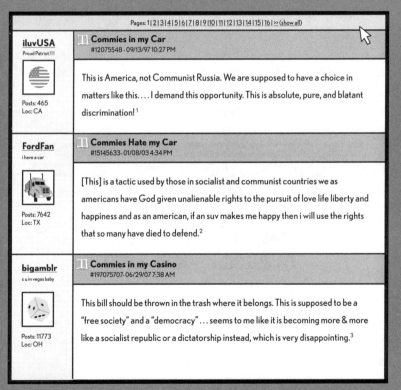

r/stopsocialism

Pages: 1|2|3|4|5|6|7|8|9|10|11|12|13|14|15|16| >> (show all)

iluvUSA
Proud Patriot!!!

Posts: 465
Loc: CA

Commies in my Car
#12075548 · 09/13/97 10:27 PM

This is America, not Communist Russia. We are supposed to have a choice in matters like this.... I demand this opportunity. This is absolute, pure, and blatant discrimination![1]

FordFan
i have a car

Posts: 7642
Loc: TX

Commies Hate my Car
#15145633 · 01/08/03 4:34 PM

[This] is a tactic used by those in socialist and communist countries we as americans have God given unalienable rights to the pursuit of love life liberty and happiness and as an american, if an suv makes me happy then i will use the rights that so many have died to defend.[2]

bigamblr
c u in vegas baby

Posts: 11773
Loc: OH

Commies in my Casino
#197075707 · 06/29/07 7:38 AM

This bill should be thrown in the trash where it belongs. This is supposed to be a "free society" and a "democracy" ... seems to me like it is becoming more & more like a socialist republic or a dictatorship instead, which is very disappointing.[3]

[1] A California resident writing to the National Highway and Traffic Safety Administration in 1997 who wanted the freedom to not have an airbag in her car.

[2] Someone whose SUV really makes them happy. But a 2003 federal proposal for fuel economy requirements was making them really sad.

[3] In 2007, this commenter really hated an online gambling regulation.

Despite what these spirited commenters believe, communism and socialism are not, in fact, implemented to deny people's freedom and independence. To the contrary, it is capitalism that has made masses of people dependent.

Associating freedom with capitalism is in the old bourgeoisie playbook. But the "freedom" that capitalists have historically advocated isn't really about freedom for the average person. Freedom meant "free trade, free selling and buying," to benefit capitalists, per The Communist Manifesto.

Even for people who want to produce a good or provide a service instead of working under someone, socialism isn't about preventing them from doing so; for Marx and Engels, it was aimed at depriving them "of the power to subjugate the labour of other" people to produce those goods and services. So, no, Dylan Musk, under socialism you will not have the freedom to gain billions of dollars by paying people poverty wages to produce, like, the Fesla.

Socialists believe there are ways to have a society that produces the things we need without exploiting workers, and they're not all coastal-elite, craft-brew-drinking hipsters. Which leads us to Myth 2.

myth 2—socialism is when bernie bros

I remember watching an American cable news show around the 2018 midterms, in which the panel of newscasters and experts could not wrap their heads around the idea that people outside of big cities like Los Angeles or New York City could want progressive policies.

Of course, socialism and progressive US policies aren't necessarily equivalent, but many of the issues progressives fight for have come from socialist and left-wing labor movements, like fighting for free universal healthcare, free public education, and living wages that relieve you from working three jobs to survive. Real radical stuff here.

But if you listen to much of mainstream media, socialists are crunchy white dudes who congregate in Bushwick coffee shops and read Jacobin all day, when they're not podcasting, obviously.

But speaking of freedom and "choice," it's not just capitalists and the petty bourgeoisie who just want the freedom to online gamble or whatever. Black people just a few generations back were deprived of the freedom to be fully human under a capitalist system. People of color in the Global South historically haven't been able to control the destiny of their own countries. Many people throughout the world, even those without a succulent plant on their windowsill (I'm dragging myself here), see a socialist or communist economy as a necessary condition for liberation, from Ghana to Jamaica to Vietnam and Bolivia.

And of course, there were Black socialist groups in the sixties in the US, such as the Republic of New Afrika, the Black Panther Party, and the Revolutionary Action Movement, founded in Ohio in 1961. Then you had all sorts of Black American leaders and creatives who were independently and explicitly socialist, communist, or vocally anti-capitalist. They're like the Mount Rushmore of Black politics, from Malcolm X and Martin Luther King to Ella Baker, Claudia Jones, and W. E. B. Du Bois (who you've already read about). There's also Angela Davis, Kathleen Cleaver, Lorraine Hansberry, Huey Newton, Bobby Seale, Fred Hampton, Paul Robeson, Bayard Rustin, and A. Philip Randolph (more on the last two in chapter 4!).

To be fair, this whitewashing of socialist history isn't totally surprising, on a practical level. As Chapter 2 touched on, white-led US labor movements (which were frequently influenced by socialists) were either apathetic or hostile to the concerns of Black Americans. And—shocker—some white socialist government leaders and organizations furthered racism, segregation, and eugenics (okay, that last one is a little bit of a shocker).

Despite the movement's sketchy record, many people of color were drawn to fundamental socialist principles anyway and formed their own radical left movements. If capitalism is considered an intrinsically American or European system, people who experienced the repression of US and European powers naturally sought the opposite, sometimes drawing from their own historically communal traditions. For them, socialism was a reprieve, a way to be self-determining and to separate their identity from the Western, capitalist countries that oppressed them.

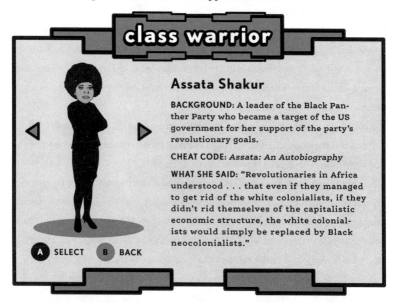

class warrior

Assata Shakur

BACKGROUND: A leader of the Black Panther Party who became a target of the US government for her support of the party's revolutionary goals.

CHEAT CODE: *Assata: An Autobiography*

WHAT SHE SAID: "Revolutionaries in Africa understood . . . that even if they managed to get rid of the white colonialists, if they didn't rid themselves of the capitalistic economic structure, the white colonialists would simply be replaced by Black neocolonialists."

A SELECT   **B** BACK

myth 3—socialism is when there is no house (or anything nice)

Capitalists want you to think theirs is the only system where you can have normal technology, personal property, or a decent house to live in. They'd have you think everyone under socialism is starving and in the

socialists:

Tweets from an iPhone

capitalists:

"Whaat I thought you all were SoCiAListS???"

socialists:

Wears clothes

capitalists:

"Ok Karl Farce, not so revolutionary after all!!"

Stone Age. Besides being deliberate misrepresentations, these myths—
that socialists want everyone to struggle, own nothing, and apparently
sew our own clothes—have legs for a reason. They likely came from a
misreading of Marx and Engels.

In The Communist Manifesto, the prolific duo called for the abolition of
"bourgeoisie private property," which has been shortened in popular
discourse to simply "private property." This has been misinterpreted
to mean the abolition of any and everyone's personal property. This, my
friends, is the socialist-to-capitalist game of Telephone.

Marx and Engels even knew that people would confuse what they were
advocating for (and they were right). We'll get into the housing issue in
Chapter 5. But before that, here's what the duo actually said about private property: "We Communists have been reproached with the desire
of abolishing the right of personally acquiring property as the fruit of a
man's own labour, which property is alleged to be the groundwork of all
personal freedom, activity, and independence.

"Hard-won, self-acquired, self-earned property! Do you mean the
property of the petty artisan and of the small peasant, a form of property that preceded the bourgeois form? There is no need to abolish that;
the development of industry has to a great extent already destroyed it,
and is still destroying it daily."

Marx and Engels didn't advocate for abolishing personal property;
they saw capitalism as doing that all on its own.

will we keep leaving socialism on "read"?

Socialism has been sliding into our DMs, even while capitalism keeps trying
to hack into our phones and block our blessings. And some of us are actually
replying. Despite all of the propaganda in capitalism's favor, more Americans

are becoming critical of capitalism and receptive to its alternatives. In June 2021, an Axios/Momentive poll of American adults showed that favorable reactions to the term capitalism went way down since 2019 (wonder why, lol), while reactions to the word socialism became more positive.

And even though there are stereotypes of socialists being white, privileged "Bernie Bros," Black people were largely driving its favorability, with Latinos right behind them. Socialism had positive connotations for 60 percent of Black Americans, 49 percent of Latinos, and 33 percent of white Americans. Black Americans were also least likely to have a positive reaction to the word capitalism. Young adults especially saw a steep drop in their positive views of capitalism.

Do you have a positive or negative reaction to the word CAPITALISM?

Race/Ethnicity	White	Black	Hispanic
Amount	1,625	265	135
positive	60%	48%	56%
negative	36%	42%	33%
rudely did not answer the question	5%	11%	11%

Do you have a positive or negative reaction to the word SOCIALISM?

Race/Ethnicity	White	Black	Hispanic
Amount	1,625	265	135
positive	33%	52%	49%
negative	61%	41%	39%
rudely did not answer the question	6%	7%	13%

Yes, there are still questions about what socialism could really look like in twenty-first-century America, or how it will work in practice—valid questions that this book will continue to explore. But we can see, right now, how capitalism fails us today and has ever since it materialized nearly two centuries ago. We've been gaslighted over and over again into staying in this truly imbalanced relationship. But fortunately, some of us are exploring our options and dating around.

If you're still holding out hope that capitalism will change, I hate to break it to you, but this is not a teen movie. While thinking you can go along and play the capitalist game, you're more likely to abandon your old friends and become cold, shiny, hard plastic than you are to actually beat the system. And everybody hates the Plastics. 💁

9 to 5

"WE ARE SOCIALISTS BECAUSE WE BELIEVE THAT WORK
MUST BE ORGANIZED FOR THE COLLECTIVE BENEFIT OF
THOSE WHO DO THE WORK AND CREATE THE PRODUCTS
AND NOT FOR THE PROFIT OF THE BOSSES"
—COMBAHEE RIVER COLLECTIVE

Listen, I know it's hard out there. If you're an aging millennial like me, this might sound familiar. You've committed to ditching the controlling, toxic players and have done everything you're supposed to do to find a good partner. At the least, you think you've got the basics down and made yourself a catch. You went to school so you can be financially stable and independent and land a good job. You learned some life skills. You've been putting work in at the gym. You're even seeing a therapist! You seriously glowed up after those awkward teen years. But after all that, you can barely get a text back.

I mean, your parents didn't need to do all that and yet they checked off all the boxes before they were thirty—they probably got married, bought a home, had a kid or two, and lived independently in their twenties.

Just like you've tried to do the right things to make room in your life for a solid relationship, you did what you thought you had to do to find a fulfilling career. While previous generations may have been able to work at one company for most of their adult lives and then collect a pension, many of today's young workers don't have that option. Many of us went to college and maybe even grad school. Yet a lot of us must work more, either at multiple jobs or somewhere super demanding and soulless, to

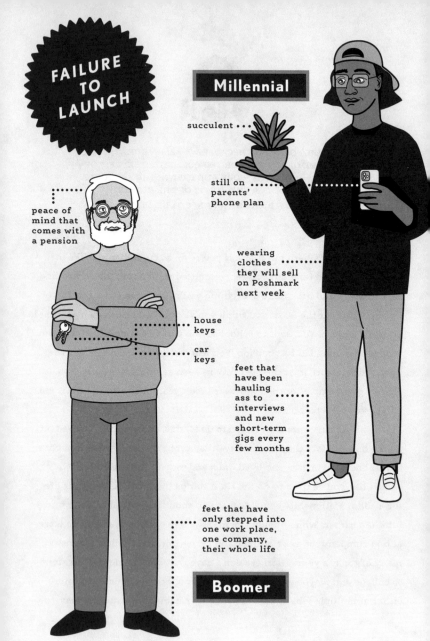

live well and to pay off student loan debt. (And by "living well," I mean renting—or, gasp, owning—your own apartment, with a washer/dryer inside of that apartment.) If we don't accomplish these things, we're told we're not hustling hard enough and that Beyoncé has the same twenty-four hours you do.

You should feel accomplished with your 9-to-5, but then you also have to deal with an asshole boss, whom you fantasize about overthrowing with a scrappy band of overworked women. You might even drive the point home with a hit country-and-western song—it's enough to drive you crazy if you let it!

This new reality for my generation, born in the past few decades—especially millennials and Gen Z—is not a happy accident. The reason things clicked more for your parents or grandparents is not because they're just better at life. Capitalism just didn't suck as hard when they were your age. Two major things have happened since the 1970s.

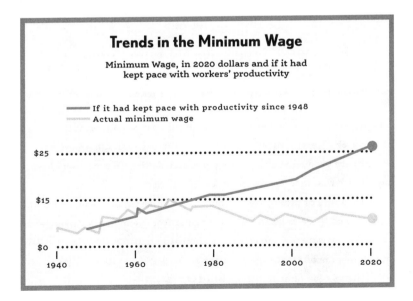

Trends in the Minimum Wage

Minimum Wage, in 2020 dollars and if it had kept pace with workers' productivity

If it had kept pace with productivity since 1948
Actual minimum wage

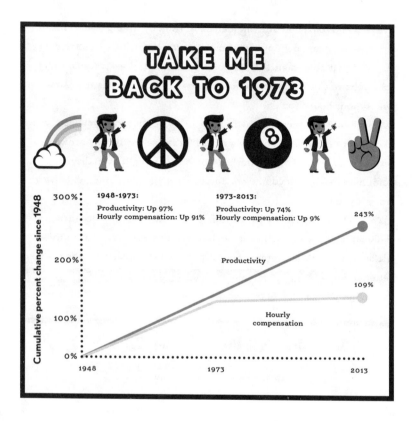

TAKE ME BACK TO 1973

Cumulative percent change since 1948

1948-1973:
Productivity: Up 97%
Hourly compensation: Up 91%

1973-2013:
Productivity: Up 74%
Hourly compensation: Up 9%

243%

300%

Productivity

200%

109%

100%

Hourly compensation

0%

1948   1973   2013

First, our wages aren't keeping up with the cost of important things—a house or childcare, for instance—and, second, even though American workers are producing even more goods and services, wages aren't keeping up with that increased production.

Your parents or grandparents could buy a home by, like, age ten (after they trekked three miles in the snow to and from elementary school, etc.) because they were making way more compared to us. In 1974, the median annual income of $11,101 would be the same as $66,415 today. But in 2020, the median annual income was $34,612.

Both the minimum wage and average hourly wages have been stagnant since the 1970s.

Americans simply aren't getting paid enough for what they do. But policymakers in the US have witnessed this dumpster fire of a situation and decided, "nah, this is fine." After generations of courtship, the marriage between capitalists and business-friendly government leaders finally eroded the labor movement. Anti-Black racism may have helped lead them down the aisle.

all taking and no giving: corporate america's increasing hostility toward labor

Big businesses in America, and the governments (both in the US and around the world) that appease them, have long been hostile to workers fighting for better working conditions and fair wages. As in, execute-labor-organizers kind of hostility.

The increasing gap between wages and productivity that came about in the 1970s is the result of legislative and policy choices; corporations finally started getting their way on a more systematic level, as union organizing and workers' bargaining power in the private sector markedly declined.

In 1954, nearly 40 percent of non-farm/non-construction workers in the United States were in a union. But some things were happening in the 1960s and early 1970s that contributed to employers' growing resistance to unions.

According to the Economic Policy Institute:

- American companies were facing global competition and felt pressure to cut costs.

- Economic power shifted to banks and investment firms, so the banks' and shareholders' needs often took precedence over those of workers.

- Profits were falling for private businesses.

Employers also began to shift to automating more industrial work and hiring more temporary workers and subcontractors—to whom they had no responsibility to provide healthcare or other benefits—leaving workers without the traditional full-time workplaces in which to build unity and organize. (See why we need free public healthcare?!)

Plenty of federal legislation and policies endorsed conservative, pro-business measures before the sixties. But in that decade willing business allies—the Supreme Court and the National Labor Relations Board, along with Republican presidents Richard Nixon, Gerald Ford, and Ronald Reagan—all got on the same page to support and amplify those laws. (We'll get to sketchy campaign donations in a later chapter.) In turn, big businesses engaged in a variety of coercive union-busting activity and intimidation tactics against labor organizing. But according to some scholarship, American public policy might not have shifted so far to the right, toward hypercapitalism, without racism.

Labor activists saw the writing on the wall that led up to this period and weren't taking these developments lightly.

Socialist Labor Activist Bayard Rustin Predicts the Future

Did you know that the full name of the 1963 March on Washington—where Dr. Martin Luther King, Jr. delivered his famous "I Have A Dream" speech—was "The March on Washington for Jobs and Freedom"?

We remember King talking about Black kids and white kids and handholding because that's what our history books focus on. I also remember (from the video footage, I wasn't alive yet) King shouting out my hometown, Stone Mountain, Georgia (woop woop!) . . . but likely because it was known for being the birthplace of the modern Ku Klux Klan (*womp womp*).

But the march was orchestrated by a pair of socialist Black labor activists, Bayard Rustin and A. Philip Randolph. The set of labor demands that Rustin announced in his speech that day are largely left out of mainstream accounts of the march. Among them he said:

"We demand that every person in this nation, black or white, be given training and work with dignity to defeat unemployment and automation."
          — **Bayard Rustin**

Yes, back in 1963, Bayard Rustin was concerned about automation. At the time, there were industrial jobs that were vulnerable to technological advances—industrial jobs that, in some cities, Black men disproportionately occupied.

In addition, Rustin called for an increase in the national minimum wage and for a government body charged with fair employment practices that would support people of color (technically he said, "Black men and other minority men"; the movement still had a ways to go with gender equality, obviously) who faced ongoing employment discrimination. Spoiler alert: His demands were not met, and his predictions for how automation would affect poorer and Black citizens largely came true.

As a disclaimer, Rustin became more conservative in his later years, especially in his foreign policy views. But his work to center labor in the civil rights movement, while organizing one of the most renowned demonstrations in history, is a reminder that the civil rights struggle was often a class struggle. ✊🏽

Although companies certainly became more politically active in the 1960s and 70s, and took advantage of weaknesses in labor law, some argue that white backlash to apparent civil rights advancements is what catalyzed the exodus of the white working class to the Republican Party, empowering pro-business, conservative politicians to steadily gut workers' power.

As sociologist G. William Domhoff argues, "the class conflict that went on in the 1960s at the legislative, regulatory, and factory levels . . . was rendered all the more volatile and difficult because white pushback against the integration of neighborhoods, schools, and workplaces was at the same time weakening the unions at the ballot box."

Domhoff continues: "It is this defection by white trade unionists from the Democrats, not the alleged sudden organization of the corporate community, which explains the right turn in the United States on labor and many other issues." Like capitalists who benefited from the anti-Black racism that grew salient during the abolitionist movement, capitalists in the 20th century were aided by backlash from white workers who opposed the calls for integration. The more things change the more things . . . you know the deal.

There is some good news, maybe (hopefully?!!). But before we get into that, let's look at how capitalist practices (e.g., looking for cheap labor) and weaker labor laws passed at the urging of powerful capitalists, of course, have royally screwed us over at our jobs.

This, my friends, is what I call ...

THE VICIOUS CYCLE OF WHY WE DON'T HAVE NICE THINGS

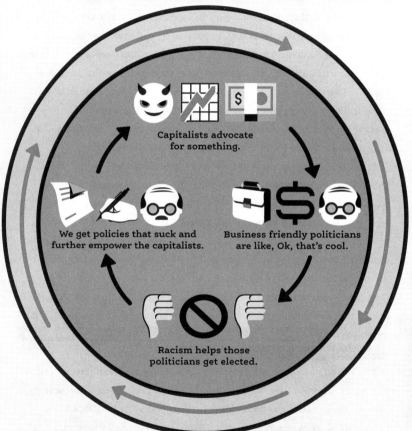

Capitalists advocate for something.

Business friendly politicians are like, Ok, that's cool.

Racism helps those politicians get elected.

We get policies that suck and further empower the capitalists.

(which can be applied to nearly every issue discussed in this book)

barely getting by: minimum wage isn't keeping up with the costs of goods and services

Even before the pandemic, there has been a long fight underway to increase the federal minimum wage, from $7.25 per hour to $15. The fact that we've even conceived of a wage that meets the bare minimum is due to capitalists, and it's a concept that has existed for over a century.

Our guys Marx and Engels (as usual) were on the case. As they said in The Communist Manifesto, the minimum wage is meant to keep workers living a bare existence as just a worker who "lives to increase capital, and is allowed to live [as] far as the interest of the ruling class requires it."

Basically, making people rely on wages that are measured to barely meet the needs of survival is bad, but given the option, capitalists will only provide the bare minimum so they can just get richer.

In the US, Congress created a national minimum wage under the Fair Labor Standards Act in 1938 to stabilize the economy after the Great Depression. It was never supposed to be the normal, average wage—it was supposed to lift people out of literal starvation. Over the years, instead of relenting and giving workers this bare minimum, many companies moved their production overseas for even cheaper labor, while other companies used their money and influence to rally up think tanks (like the Employment Policies Institute) and lobbyists (like the National Restaurant Association) to keep the federal government from raising it any higher. If all of this looks bad for the average American worker, just consider the racial disparities on top of that.

Black men have been hit harder by the decline in manufacturing, with one study showing that "[o]ne-third of the increase in wage inequality among black men is due to manufacturing decline" from 1960–2010.

Overall, the economic outlook for Black workers (and those who can't find work) in formerly industrial cities in the Midwest that were once highly unionized is worse than anywhere else in the country.

The Price of Cheap Labor

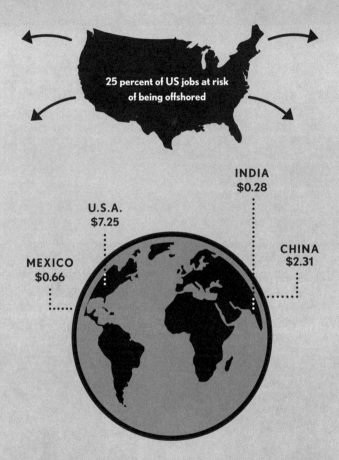

25 percent of US jobs at risk of being offshored

INDIA
$0.28

U.S.A.
$7.25

CHINA
$2.31

MEXICO
$0.66

In 2021, China's largest province had a minimum hourly wage of $2.31 USD, India had minimum wage of $0.28 USD, and Mexico had a minimum wage of $0.66 USD. Whereas, the minimum wage in the US was $7.25 (which is still insanely low and unlivable and is the same as what it was when I was in high school—and I'm an *old* millennial, okay.)

The world's billionaires made $5 trillion from 2021–2022 and the ten richest men in the world doubled their collective income. The growth in wealth has been so great over such a short period of time that "wealth concentration at the very top now surpasses the peak of the Gilded Age of the late 19th century," Oxfam says.

Uber driver

33 percent of work is temporary work or gigs that limit benefits but require the same hours as full employment.

From 2014–2018, the annual median income for Black Milwaukeeans, for instance, was worse than any other major city in the country, with Black households making just 42 percent of what white households made. That's if they can even find work. In eleven major US cities from 2014–2018, at least 30 percent of Black men in their prime working years were jobless.

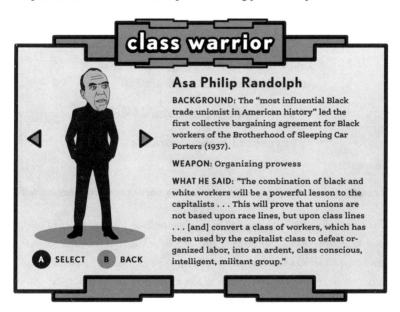

class warrior

Asa Philip Randolph

BACKGROUND: The "most influential Black trade unionist in American history" led the first collective bargaining agreement for Black workers of the Brotherhood of Sleeping Car Porters (1937).

WEAPON: Organizing prowess

WHAT HE SAID: "The combination of black and white workers will be a powerful lesson to the capitalists . . . This will prove that unions are not based upon race lines, but upon class lines . . . [and] convert a class of workers, which has been used by the capitalist class to defeat organized labor, into an ardent, class conscious, intelligent, militant group."

A SELECT   **B** BACK

covid capitalism

Now, all of this was brewing well before COVID came into the mix, which left millions of workers of color even more vulnerable. Meanwhile, corporate bosses and politicians guilted people into going back to work just weeks into the deadly pandemic, if they even allowed their workers to stay home in the first place. In New York City, which was initially ground zero for the pandemic in the US, COVID impacted workers of color especially hard.

> ## 75 percent of "essential workers" overall during the pandemic in NYC were Black, Latino, or Asian, including:
>
> - **80 percent of building cleaners**
> - **77 percent of trucking, warehouse, and postal service workers**
> - **74 percent of grocery store workers**
> - **71 percent of transit workers**

But not long after, like the "Mission Accomplished" banner raised behind President George W. Bush in the middle of the Iraq War, the propaganda that Americans were winning the war on coronavirus was already in full effect. It was time to return to life as normal. Primarily, "life" in this usage meant "a job that you probably hate a little bit."

And like a misguided general leading their troops into a war, some elected officials argued that it was our patriotic duty to labor in a disease-infested workplace. Meanwhile those elected officials were safely working from home, though occasionally breaking quarantine to have fancy super-spreader cocktail events.

These are the grand delusions of capitalism. Though, to be clear, the bosses aren't deluded at all. They were hoping concerns about whether we lived or died would take a backseat to concerns about the economic health of rich investors.

exploring our options

Finally, here's some good news: first, there has been a ton of labor organizing over the past few years, much of it sparked by the grotesque inequality we saw even more keenly during the pandemic. Secondly, there are now other ways we can reorganize our workplace that get at the heart of capitalist exploitation.

While corporate heads were busy engaging in wartimelike propaganda to rally employees against the threat of COVID-19, they didn't notice that an impromptu class war was underway among the ranks of regular American workers.

During what became known as the "Great Resignation," millions of people quit their jobs at record rates. From July–December 2021, over 4 million people quit their jobs each month, with food service and retail workers leading the charge. Fewer people felt compelled to stay in a crappy work relationship. At the same time, other workers were raising their standards and demanding more from the jobs they had. Cornell University identified 1,700 labor protests and strikes from March 2020–August 2022.

The pandemic highlighted how ruthless capitalists can be—and how great the power of workers can be when they decide they won't just take it.

Labor movement energy has continued even as the pandemic slowed. There's the early success of the Amazon Labor Union (more on that in Chapter 10!); nurses in New York who won pay raises after striking in early 2023, hundreds of Starbucks workers who have voted to unionize, and the 2022 California law for fast-food workers that enhances their power to bargain and negotiate for better wages (which only came to pass after a decade of worker organizing). All this activity has likely only made the labor movement more popular: American approval of labor unions was higher in 2022 than it's been since 1965.

white-washing america's workers

The rise of the current labor movement can be partly attributed to the broader recognition that the working class is not just a stereotype of blue-collar workers from yesteryear, i.e., some white, male factory worker in Michigan.

The whitewashing of the working class has irked me to no end, and I've talked about it at length in my reporting if you want more details and tirades. But it's important to note here that this isn't a new phenomenon.

Treating the "working class" or the working poor as synonymous with white people, and erasing Black people from our conception of who's a worker—and therefore deserving of adequate economic policy—is a problem even W. E. B. Du Bois examined. He called out the media's framing of Black people in particular after the Civil War. In *Black Reconstruction in America*, published in 1935, he wrote:

"The newspapers specialized on news that flattered the poor whites and almost utterly ignored the Negro except in crime and ridicule. . . . The result of this was that the wages of both classes could be kept low, the whites fearing to be supplanted by Negro labor, the Negros always being threatened by the substitution of white labor."

– W. E. B. Du Bois

The working class includes Black and Latino warehouse workers. Asian grocery store clerks. Women nurses. Rideshare drivers. Teachers, call-center employees, and domestic workers. Organizing a multiracial working class—and not just centering white workers—is the only foreseeable way to defeat the seemingly insurmountable challenges capitalists constantly throw at the labor movement.

To be sure, getting concessions from capitalists is not the end-goal of socialism. Replacing them is. But, in the meantime, people gotta eat. And like, it would be cool to live without constant struggle.

So what does an alternative to the capitalist workplace look like?

One option is the Worker Self-Directed Enterprise, a term coined by Richard Wolff, considered America's most prominent Marxist economist.

In a WSDE, a "collective of workers that produces a surplus (i.e., a profit) gathers to collectively receive that surplus and distribute it. The surplus is never appropriated and distributed by others." Basically, unlike your average corporation, you don't have a small group of employers deciding how to spend the profit that employees produce. Furthermore, the bigwigs in the C-suites aren't unilaterally making management decisions, like deciding to move a company out of town to places with weak labor laws. Instead, workers decide democratically how to manage the company.

I talked to him more about WSDEs and his vision for the ideal workplace. Just imagine that I was nodding my head furiously as he talked like it was Sunday service.

Richard Wolff's Democratic Vision of Labor

IMAGINE A PLACE WHERE, Monday through Thursday, you come into work like you always have. And on Friday, you come to work, but you don't do your normal thing. Friday is devoted to meetings, where you discuss the basic problems of your business. "Are some of our products not selling well? Are we getting sick on the job?" Whatever the basic issues are, you get together and you collectively decide what the problems are and what you're gonna do about them.

If there are options, you choose democratically—one person, one vote. Every person now has two job descriptions. Whatever the particular activity you do, that's one of your job descriptions. Here's the other one: you have to be at those meetings on Friday, you have to learn about the problems this enterprise has.

You will be a leader, you're going to be a decider, you're going to be part of what runs this enterprise, because that's as fundamental to this enterprise as your regular job was before. In those days, they said to you, "if you don't do this particular task, we will fire you."

Well, in the co-op world, you're going to discover that each person has capabilities they didn't know about, that each has new skills to learn and apply. Because if we can find things that you're really good at, that you didn't even know about or didn't ever develop, then it becomes in the interest of the community to help you develop those skills, because you'll be a happier, better contributor to that community. We want this job to be something you look forward to going to five days a week—not dreading it, not looking at the clock on the wall, waiting for when lunchtime comes.

We want a socialist workplace to be a place of learning, of creativity, of people developing and changing. In this vision, you don't work in order to live. In a socialist community, we're going to sustain you to live in any case. What we want is for you to be a creative, enthusiastic, interested person. And therefore, developing you is the best thing we can do for all of us. And that's why the workplace is going to be a completely different experience from the horror you live through now.

What the workplace looks like under a socialist economy is, in part, what its workers decide it looks like, with the fundamental understanding (and some legal parameters) that they are all paid fairly for their labor and not merely paid what capitalists decide in their boardrooms. But Wolff, Akuno, and many other socialists cite Spain's Mondragon federation of worker cooperatives as an example of how this works. It's the seventh-largest corporation in Spain and has more than 100,000 workers. As Wolff shares, the Mondragon Corporation is a "family of about two hundred co-ops that are all under one corporate umbrella. They are all closet socialists. They'll tell you 'we try to avoid getting too much wrapped up in politics.' But when they say that, they wink. If the workers are not happy with the supervisors, they have meetings, and they can decide whether to keep the supervisor or not. In other words, the supervisors don't hire the workers; it's the other way around.

"Managers aren't paid more than six times what the lowest paid worker makes, unlike our current capitalist system in the US where the average gap between a CEO's pay and the median worker is 670-to-1."

As the late socialist activist Bruce A. Dixon describes in *Jackson Rising*:

When a Mondragon factory or store or other operation has to close because of unprofitability, Mondragon retrains and relocates those workers to other cooperative enterprises. . . . they're about to offer their own MBA program, to guarantee that they get trained managers without the bloodsucking, predatory mindset taught and valued at most business schools. ✊

can we find a whole new way to make a living?

It's fair to wonder if a key feature of capitalism—owners employing wage labor and amassing more and more profits from them—can be largely replaced. And where this change is needed the most (in the US, given its vast income and wealth inequality), it is probably the most difficult to accomplish, politically. We couldn't even agree to put on masks in a pandemic!

But I always think about how US abolitionists felt when our ancestors were still enslaved. Chattel slavery wasn't just a physical or economic phenomenon. It was psychological. Capitalists and racists (not mutually exclusive) tried to convince the world that Black people weren't even fully human and thus were not deserving of freedom. After a couple of centuries, it would have been easy for everyone to believe this was a scientific truth. But revolutionaries were born who refused to accept this mythology. Americans also have to want a change. We can talk to our friends all day about the benefits of another relationship, or at least about leaving the one we're currently in and frustrated with. But ultimately, we have to choose to actually walk away, into some uncertainty.

If we hold on stubbornly to the status quo because of some nominal benefits and treat capitalism as inevitable, it will be. But if we keep chipping away at capitalism's myths, we can find freedom for future generations, and maybe even our own. In the (paraphrased) words of the great Dolly Parton, the tide can turn, and it can all roll our way. 🐝

5

Don't Call Me on My Cellphone

"WE BELIEVE THAT THE GOVERNMENT MUST
PROVIDE, FREE OF CHARGE, FOR THE PEOPLE,
HEALTH FACILITIES THAT WILL NOT ONLY TREAT
OUR ILLNESSES, MOST OF WHICH ARE A RESULT
OF OUR OPPRESSION, BUT THAT WILL ALSO
DEVELOP PREVENTATIVE MEDICAL PROGRAMS
TO GUARANTEE OUR FUTURE SURVIVAL."
—BLACK PANTHER PARTY
PROGRAM PLATFORM, MARCH 1972

Okay, we're making progress. You left that abusive job and got a union
position at a company that tries to share decision-making collectively
and actually respect everyone's time. You start getting over the past,
being all healthy and going out more, running out of pages in your
passport. And then BOOM. Your ex slides into your DMs. Again. It's like
they have an antenna that knows when you've gotten over them and
gotten it together, and they whine about you going to places they think
you don't belong.

This is what all those ads decrying Medicare for All felt like during the
2020 election. They are the Drake in our lives, raising a fit because we're
trying to move on. We were bombarded with multimillion-dollar campaigns telling us that life couldn't possibly be better with public healthcare—there would be no choice and no freedom!—precisely because
so many people were finally so over America's current for-profit
healthcare system.

HEALTHCARE HUSTLE

Sees you healthy, prospering, and getting exactly what you need without them

Successfully convinces you that you actually still need them

Even while pundits have always framed Medicare for All as a radical idea, in the 2020 Democratic primary in South Carolina (a state widely known for its radical-left revolutionaries and Commies), more voters supported "replacing all private health insurance with a single government plan for everyone" than those who opposed it.

THE MATH ISN'T MATHING

87% of Democrats support Medicare for All	**+**	41% of people have negative views of private insurance	**+** A pandemic that leaves COVID-19 hospital patients with an average $50,000 medical bill	**=** Absolutely nothing changes

The idea of free, government-funded healthcare is growing in popularity. But like with many of our social services, we can only have good things in limited ways or in temporary spurts, with the ever-looming threat that they will end. Probably like how Jimmy Brooks felt when his basketball dreams were dashed halfway into the season. (But maybe we can eventually get that good Dutch healthcare and piece it back together like Jimmy did in those later Degrassi seasons??)

universal health care and single-payer healthcare 101

Universal healthcare means that "all individuals and communities receive the health services they need without suffering financial hardship."

Single-payer healthcare is one type of universal healthcare where "rather than multiple competing health insurance companies, a single public or quasi-public agency takes responsibility for financing healthcare for all residents," so everyone has health insurance under one health insurance plan "and has access to necessary services—including doctors, hospitals, long-term care, prescription drugs, dentists and vision care."

Single-payer healthcare is often funded by taxes. Medicare in the United States—which 2020 presidential candidates Bernie Sanders and Elizabeth Warren wanted to make universal via "Medicare for All"—is funded both by taxes and by additional funding authorized by Congress. The Medicare for All plan would have generated most of its revenue from increasing taxes paid by large employers.

We're not lacking universal, free public healthcare in order to teach us all "personal responsibility." The government's reason for limiting our social safety net is often framed this way, as if we are children without self-control who need a gazillion-dollar hospital bill and a "choice" of insurers to be real adults (even though most people have no real choice—their employers likely offer one insurance provider and two or three plans, tops. Oh, and the unemployed are screwed, obviously).

The reality is that a lot of big companies with a vested interest in making money off our basic human need for healthcare have immense influence on government officials.

For brief moments during the coronavirus pandemic, we saw what a coordinated healthcare system that minimized costs could look like, with hospitalization waivers, free COVID tests, free vaccines, and subsidies for COBRA (a government-sponsored program that allows employees to continue health coverage for a limited time when they leave a job). The $1.9 trillion American Rescue Plan (ARP) temporarily provided a lifeline for those on the edge of economic collapse. But as Pulitzer Prize–winning journalist Chris Hedges noted:

> [T]he ARP will not alter the structural inequities, either by raising the minimum wage to $15 an hour or imposing taxes and regulations on corporations or the billionaire class that saw its wealth increase by a staggering $1.1 trillion since the start of the pandemic.
>
> The health system will remain privatized, meaning the insurance and pharmaceutical corporations will reap a windfall of tens of billions of dollars with the ARP, and this when they are already making record profits.

why we have for-profit healthcare

Fortunately for health insurance companies and their fat pockets, conservative politicians and elites in the US have stoked fears of desegregation and socialism to keep the rest of us from having a universal single-payer healthcare plan.

This didn't just start in the past few decades, and it certainly didn't start when young people starting "feeling the Bern." It's been this way since the first proposals for nationalized health insurance started to pop up, in the early 1900s.

We've been talking about
NATIONAL
forevvverrr . . .

1912
Teddy Roosevelt proposes national health insurance under Progressive Party platform.

Around WWI, 1914–1918
US government commissioned articles denouncing German socialist insurance as part of their anti-German war propaganda, leading government health insurance to appear "anti-American."

1915
American Association of Labor Legislation drafts model bill for insurance that covers the services of physicians, nurses, and hospitals, as well as sick pay, maternity benefits, and a death benefit for funeral expenses. Workers, employers, and the state would share the costs. Multimillion-dollar commercial life insurance industry opposes the bill and it dies.

HEALTHCARE

1940s-1950s
National Medical Association, an organization of Black medical professionals, frames healthcare as a human right and supports national healthcare proposals, in direct opposition to the American Medical Association, which continues to argue against national health insurance program.

2010
The most significant healthcare reform we've gotten this century has been the Affordable Care Act, which President Barack Obama signed into law in March 2010. Despite conservative attempts to frame it as "socialized medicine," ACA was mostly about regulating the private health insurance market and requiring that most Americans get covered.

1940s
Harry Truman introduces a national health insurance program and links healthcare with civil rights. The American Medical Association—which excluded Black members—calls national health insurance un-American, because "states' rights." Southern Democrats raise alarms that it would desegregate the medical profession and usher in socialism. Just see the next two pages.

1961-1965
President John F. Kennedy makes Medicare for the elderly a legislative priority. It ultimately passed in 1965 during the Johnson administration, against conservative opposition, and is still in place (and hugely popular) today.

a (near) replica of an
actual AMA brochure:

THE _VOLUNTARY_ WAY IS
THE AMERICAN WAY

"In all that the people can individually do
as well for themselves, government ought
not to interfere." — ABRAHAM LINCOLN

HEALTH INSURANCE

Compulsory or Voluntary

The people's decision will determine the ultimate fate of Freedom and Truth in this Nation.

You May Be Next!

Q. Would socialized medicine lead to socialization of other phases of American life?

A. Lenin thought so. According to Lawrence Sullivan in his book *The Case Against Socialized Medicine*, the founder of international revolutionary Communism once proclaimed socialized medicine "the keystone of the arch of the Socialist State."

Today, much of the world has launched out on that road. If the medical profession should be socialized because people need doctors, *why not the milk industry*? Certainly, more people need milk every day than need doctors.

On the same erroneous premise, *why not the corner grocery*? Adequate diet is the very basis of good health!

Why not nationalize lawyers, miners, businessmen, farmers? Germany did, Russia did. England is in the process.

Opposition to a national health plan went into high gear during the Cold War and continued beyond it, with prominent public figures fear-mongering about it destroying the American way of life. Have you ever dated someone who condescendingly says they know what's best for you, as if you can't trust your own judgment? That's been our history with single-payer healthcare.

very chill reactions from the right about rAdIcAl healthcare plans

"The democracy of our republic is threatened by the steady encroachment of socialistic, bureaucratic government. What began as an apparently innocent effort for comfort and happiness is becoming a destructive instrument of dictatorship."	"The welfare state . . . is that state of twilight in which the glow of democratic freedoms is fading beyond the horizon, leaving us to be swallowed in the blackness of socialism or worse."	"This program, I promise you, will pass just as surely as the sun will come up tomorrow; and behind it will come other federal programs that will invade every area of freedom as we have known it in this country. Until, one day, as Norman Thomas said, we will awake to find that we have socialism."	"I will not endorse nor go with a nationalized [plan]—they used to say socialized medicine— that will guarantee only long lines, indifferent service, and very high taxes."
American Medical Association president **ERNEST IRONS** in 1950, basically equating President Harry Truman's national healthcare plan to a Russian gulag or something.	Senator **HARRY BYRD** (D-VA), also being super dramatic about President Truman's plan for national health insurance and other social programs, in 1952	**RONALD REAGAN**—then an actor commissioned by the American Medical Association for a PR campaign— having a normal one describing the precursor to Medicare in 1961	**GEORGE H. W. BUSH** making up things to the staff of the University Medical Center of Southern Nevada, in 1992

So basically, not that different from Republicans today—and certain cable news networks—screaming "SOCIALISM!!" every five minutes, as single-payer healthcare becomes more popular than ever. There's a long legacy with this mess. And conveniently, none of these men even bother to say why socialism would be so bad for people's health and well-being. (And btw the USSR was arguably not socialist—some would say it wasn't even communist.)

the high price of insuring our health

Coincidentally (but not a coincidence at all), equating government-run national healthcare with an un-American, nuclear-armed threat aligned with the financial interests of private insurers.

As historian Christy Ford Chapin notes, companies belonging to the Health Insurance Association of America (HIAA), founded in 1956, exerted a lot of behind-the-scenes political pressure to build the private insurance company model, even though they knew it wouldn't be the most effective system and could lead to rising medical costs.

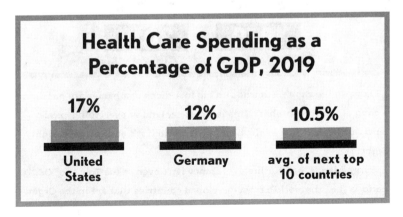

Health Care Spending as a Percentage of GDP, 2019

17%
United States

12%
Germany

10.5%
avg. of next top 10 countries

And rise they did. Data shows that health spending in the US has increased thirty-fold in the last four decades or, adjusting for inflation, from $1,848 per person in 1970 to $11,582 in 2019.

The technical term for this is: absolute clusterfuck.

In the US, we spend more on healthcare per capita than any other wealthy country by far, and it continues to grow over time.

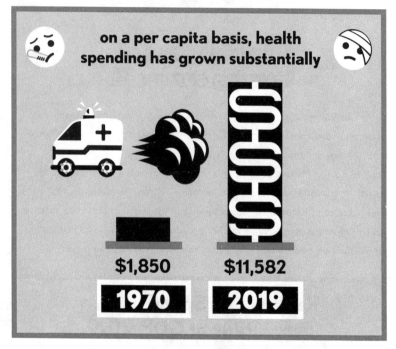

on a per capita basis, health spending has grown substantially

$1,850 — **1970**

$11,582 — **2019**

Okay, so the capitalists who run big insurance companies are pocketing a gang of money. So what? This is America, land of everything excellent. Our health must be the best in the world if it's so expensive, right? Right????

Sorry friends, but our life expectancy isn't even in the Top 25 of OECD nations (i.e., the world's most developed countries that are in the Organisation for Economic Co-operation and Development). The average man won't live past the age of 74.2, which is the thirty-second best life expectancy for men out of forty-nine countries. Women's life expectancy in the US is the thirty-fourth best, at 79.9 years.

Of the world's most developed nations, only three countries fare worse in infant mortality rates.

And our for-profit, insurance-based system isn't incentivizing more doctors to practice either. Among OECD countries, the US has one of the lowest numbers of practicing physicians per 1,000 people (2.6 physicians), giving us the thirteenth worst rate out of sixteen countries.

Despite all this, we keep swiping right on America's healthcare system.

If you've read each chapter of this book thus far, you may already have a clue what I'm about to say next. If this is the state of our health in general, it is not looking pretty when you take race into account.

Why Are We Swiping Right on This?

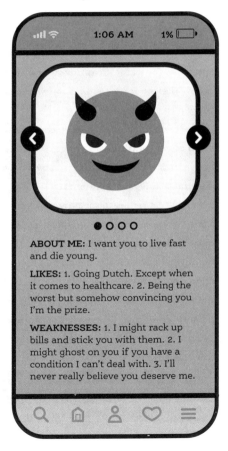

ABOUT ME: I want you to live fast and die young.

LIKES: 1. Going Dutch. Except when it comes to healthcare. 2. Being the worst but somehow convincing you I'm the prize.

WEAKNESSES: 1. I might rack up bills and stick you with them. 2. I might ghost on you if you have a condition I can't deal with. 3. I'll never really believe you deserve me.

race, class, and . . . eugenics?? oh my.

Because capitalists and other elites transformed race into something biological and immutable, racism has affected practically every aspect of our lives, including our health.

So even if we had a government-funded, single-payer healthcare system—which we absolutely need and should fight for—it wouldn't undo the centuries of racist practices and policies that facilitated poor health outcomes for a significant number of people of color and some white people (i.e., poor whites who were conceptualized as being a separate, pauper "race").

These are policies that have led to more white Americans living in areas of concentrated affluence, while Blacks and Latinos are more likely to live in areas of concentrated poverty where there is more exposure to harmful toxins and pollutants.

In its 2003 report *Unequal Treatment: Confronting Racial and Ethnic Disparities in Healthcare*, the National Academies' Institute of Medicine "reviewed more than 100 studies and concluded that bias, prejudice, and stereotyping contributed to widespread differences in healthcare by race and ethnicity." Fifteen years later, a 2018 study found that "Black, American Indian and Alaska Native, and Native Hawaiian and Pacific Islander patients continued to receive poorer care than White patients on 40 percent of the quality measures included, with little to no improvement from decades past."

In the same way we arrived at capitalism through both a series of policies and brute force, today's disparities in people's health don't exist by happenstance. This sad state of affairs largely came from a set of beliefs of a wealthy, powerful minority, and they turned those beliefs into professional practices and public policy—and some of those beliefs are f&*%($! BONKERS. (For the baby leftists that might be reading this, the censored word is "totally.")

We haven't quite been stuck in the same cycle of racism and capitalism that led to these health outcomes, since explicit racists are considered extremists nowadays. But there is a definite race/class evolution that got us here.

Those health disparities are used to justify why capitalists and the state shouldn't care about the working class's health problems anyway.

Southern physician

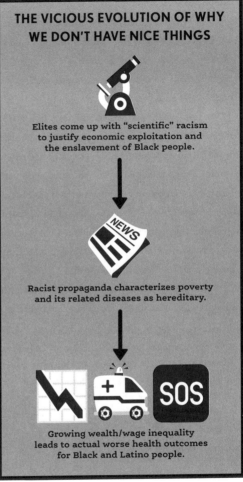

THE VICIOUS EVOLUTION OF WHY WE DON'T HAVE NICE THINGS

Elites come up with "scientific" racism to justify economic exploitation and the enslavement of Black people.

Racist propaganda characterizes poverty and its related diseases as hereditary.

Growing wealth/wage inequality leads to actual worse health outcomes for Black and Latino people.

Samuel Cartwright is one of those elites who made up BS to justify Black people's enslavement. In 1851, writing in a New Orleans medical journal, he invented illnesses "peculiar to negroes." One was *drapetomania*, a disease he claimed caused enslaved Africans to flee from captivity. As the New England Journal of Medicine noted, Cartwright argued that it could be prevented by keeping Black people in submission and could be cured by whippings. Cartwright also "discovered" *dysaesthesia aethiopica*, "a 'disease' in Black people characterized by reduced intellectual ability, laziness, and partial insensitivity of the skin."

This has repercussions to this day. In a 2016 study of racial attitudes, "half of White medical students and residents held unfounded beliefs about intrinsic biologic differences between Black people and White people. These false beliefs were associated with assessments of Black patients' pain as being less severe than that of White patients and with less appropriate treatment decisions for Black patients."

In his book on scientific racism, *The Legacy of Malthus*, reporter Allan Chase observed that scientific racism was simply concerned with maximizing profits and minimizing the taxation of those profits.

He also dropped this dime about how scientific racism came about when religion was being used less frequently to blame people for their problems:

> Scientific racism did not, obviously, invent the reluctance to pay living wages and taxes for the promotion of the general welfare of an entire nation's people. It did, however, appear at a critical turn in history when the classic scriptural excuses for greed, selfishness, and poverty were fast losing their traditional credibility . . . [so scientific racism] became the rationale in the rapidly industrializing nations of Europe and, shortly, North America.

Now ain't that some s--t.

Heading into the turn of the century, there was also a growing belief in eugenics, a pseudoscientific movement that sought to breed the perfect race (i.e., white, Anglo-Saxon). White medical professionals and policy makers used similar arguments as those from the Industrial Revolution, expressing apathy or even disdain at the prospect of improving health outcomes of Black Americans and poor whites.

As historian Karen Kruse Thomas shows, the president of the American Medical Association's North Carolina chapter, Hubert Haywood, went so far as to argue that Black people and poor whites were biologically inferior and more susceptible to disease, so national health insurance that included those groups would be a waste of money.

And it gets worse.

HAYWOOD ARGUED THAT:

Black people simply existing would have an "adverse effect on the white race," he noted in a 1941 speech, because Black blood would filter into the white population.	
Empathy and adequate social services for Black Americans intervened with nature's plan: the extinction of the Black race.	
So keeping Black people healthy was both futile and dangerous.	

Overall, in the South, as Thomas documents, "white doctors viewed socialized medicine as a threat to two of their most cherished ideals: segregation and physician autonomy."

The AMA, of which many of these doctors were a part, influenced conservative policy makers and facilitated a defeat of President Truman's national health insurance plan.

Clearly, untangling ourselves from the messy, atrocious web of racist lies, anti-socialist propaganda, and corporate influence on our healthcare will take a lot of work. Like, probably a revolution. But you're only five chapters in so maybe you're not ready for all that. So I'll just say we need to radically transform the system, because this. is. not. working.

so how do we get the health care we need?

With Medicare for All, we had a ready-made bill to create another model, but for now it's still just on paper. But we've seen how other systems—that rely much less on for-profit insurers—work in real life. Take Spain's National Health System. It'll make you swoon.

HOW IT WORKS IN SPAIN:

- Universal, single-payer system guaranteed as a constitutional right and financed through taxes. About 99.1 percent of the population is covered, and 15 percent purchase additional private health insurance.

- Almost all covered services are free, except dental care is mostly out of pocket, and prescription drugs use a co-payment system.

- The Spanish government creates laws and regulations to keep pharmaceutical companies in check so they don't charge absurd prices, making them one of the most highly regulated industries in the country.

- Patients can choose their primary care physician (which is called a general practitioner in Europe) and their nurse.

Okay, so the government handles their healthcare. But don't people have to wait in absurdly long lines to be treated? Are they even that healthy?

Contrary to George H. W. Bush's warning about "socialized medicine" in the 1990s, unmet medical care needs relating to cost, distance, or waiting times were reported by only 0.2 percent of Spain's population in 2019, well below the EU average of 1.7 percent. And in 2019 (before COVID-19), Spanish life expectancy of eighty-four years was one of the highest among high-income countries in the world (and was five years longer than that of the US, which was at this same time 78.8).

The big problem in the US, though, isn't envisioning another system. As I said, we've been discussing these alternatives for a literal century. It's political will, that's the problem. Our elected officials just can't get out of the insurance companies' beds, even if the people are back out in the field. But there's also this pretty big issue of people not electing representatives who will push for policy like Medicare for All, even if they say they want it. I asked Nina Turner—the former Ohio state senator and chair of Bernie Sanders's PAC, Our Revolution—how to get around that.

"It really is going to take a grassroots organizing effort to go into communities and help them to see the vision that it can actually happen," she says. Yes, reader, that good ol' organizing we hear so much about. But it's one of the few tools leftists have to combat the huge propaganda machine we know capitalists have at their disposal.

Turner speaks to that point: "I think the neoliberal class has done a very good job of convincing the people in this country to not suspend their disbelief and make them think that they don't deserve better than what they're getting," she shares. "And so we got to fight those messages."

That organizing is already happening, so it's not like you have to pop up at a stranger's house unannounced. "For example," Turner notes, "National Nurses United has been advocating for universal healthcare for a very long time." From personal experience, I can verify that they have organizing calls, texting campaigns (that I've received *plenty of times*) and demonstrations to advocate for Medicare for All.

And while the federal government is necessary to institute single-payer healthcare on the national level, there are also state-level Medicare for All policies and campaigns in the works that people can fight for, including a Medicare for All law in California. Turner adds:

> "Once one state does it, [it increases] the likelihood that other states will follow suit, [but] it goes back to the type of people that you elect. There's no guarantee that just because a majority of the people want something that we get it. We the people have to make elected officials do these things. And if they don't, we have to let them know that there's going to be a consequence for not adhering to our will."

Not to be all bootstrappy in a book on socialism, but we really do have some responsibility in getting the kind of relationship we want. We always hear about communication and expressing our needs with our partners. Well, we've got to take it a step further and stand by our deal-breakers when it comes to who we put in power to represent us. And if our representatives are being noncommittal on single-payer healthcare, it's up to us to move on.

Just imagine what could happen when we do leave for better options.

Access to a quality physician wouldn't depend on where we live or how much money we make. We might be more vigilant about seeking treatment before we get really ill because we wouldn't be afraid of the hospital bill. People wouldn't fall into debt and bankruptcy just to take care of themselves.

And beyond health outcomes, maybe we could actually save up and take time off from work to explore other interests and hobbies because we wouldn't be afraid of losing our healthcare to do that. (As I write this, I'm in fact walking around without healthcare, because it was practically impossible to finish this book and keep my full-time job that gave me health insurance.)

Given America's history of racism, better health is also not limited to a state-funded healthcare plan. It requires a fundamentally different economic system and an investment in Black people and other Americans who have faced an intergenerational avalanche of racist practices and policies coming from a government and society that cared very little if they lived or died.

Capitalism and racism have been working together to keep us sick and straggly. We've been stuck with them for so long we think this is just how we're supposed to look and feel. When we periodically look in the mirror and realize something is wrong, they magically hit up our phone line and play the same ol' song, probably one from a Toronto rapper, about how we don't need nobody else.

If anything, let's advocate for socialism so we can continue our glow-up and send these greedy capitalists straight to voicemail. ✊🏾

6

Keeping Up with the Joneses

"WITNESSING THE HORRIBLE POVERTY HERE AND THE MILLIONS OF PEOPLE WHO HAVE NO WORK, FOOD, OR HOME . . . IN THIS COUNTRY OF SCUMBAG MILLIONAIRES, WHO GREEDILY GRAB EVERYTHING, HAS PROFOUNDLY SHOCKED US."
—FRÍDA KAHLO

In the world of love—not that I'm such a genius at it—mixed signals suck (that whole back and forth with Nia Long and Larenz Tate in *Love Jones*, anyone?) Yeah, yeah, mixed signals mean "no." But we're human after all and like to believe we can wish something into existence. We're craving a loving relationship, and we want this person to be The One. If we just change one thing up, or maybe just stick around a little longer, then maybe something can grow out of this rollercoaster situationship.

This is what homeownership feels like in the United States.

There are some good things about it. Some bad things about it. Ultimately, getting everyone to own a home isn't a socialist solution to our housing crisis. However, we should all have the option to afford to live where and how we want.

And, unlike the myths you may have heard, owning property doesn't make you a capitalist. As we discussed in Chapter 3, Marx and Engels weren't referring to the average person's home (for those who can afford one) when they talked about abolishing private property. The main issue they had was bourgeois property, i.e., capitalists owning factories, land, and other property used to exploit other people's labor.

Though, as Engels argued, being a homeowner might suck if you ever needed to strike and protest your work conditions, since you might be less likely to go on strike and confront your capitalist bosses. After investing

The Chart of Conflicted Feelings

OKAY THIS IS COOL	OH NO, ABORT MISSION!
Buying a home can provide financial stability for a lot of people, and can serve as built-in rent stabilization, as someone on Twitter told me (shout out to @PontiousPilate). This is fair, seeing how landlords can raise your rent each year, but with a fixed-rate mortgage your monthly payment is locked in.	Homeownership as a source of asset building also requires a for-profit market that tends to discriminate against non-homeowners and deepen inequality and individualism. Like how your mom's next-door neighbor Sue (it would be a Sue) went to the zoning meeting to rant against building affordable housing or approving a bus stop nearby because they lower property values? That kind of individualism.
Home ownership creates intergenerational wealth for many Americans, including the working class.	Explicitly racist housing policies and business practices have made homeownership much less valuable for many people of color, if it's attainable at all, given how property values have grown exponentially without much increase in wages. We have actual lawyers (me) who can't comfortably afford a decent condo in their home city (like mine) because the market is doing market things and investors are jacking up prices (I'm not crying, you're crying).
For many southern Blacks especially, after generations of sharecropping and being forced into deplorable housing conditions, owning land and a home could offer independence and necessary comfort and security in a hostile, anti-Black world.	Black homeowners are still displaced and housing insecure, after a long history of racial terror, discrimination, wealth extraction, eminent domain policies, and neoliberal deregulation that has forced many of us out of our homes and communities. Y'know, just super casual stuff that the right wing *totally* wants us to learn about in public school and neighbor Sue is absolutely *not* trying to ban from the curriculum.

in a home, who wants to risk losing an income and not being able to afford your mortgage? (And I would argue that having a 30,000-square-foot mansion, however you earned it, isn't a particularly good thing.)

In the twenty-first century, rent has gotten out of hand and many people probably would like the stability and potential affordability of homeownership. Whatever you think about Marx's argument, we also know that a profit-driven real estate market incentivizes a focus on large returns and treats homes as any other investment—a way to grow wealth, not just to live safely and securely. This leads to all sorts of social and economic problems.

Because of that, and the fact that owning a home isn't the key to racial equality that many might believe it to be, I have conflicting feelings about the push for homeownership under capitalism—especially in the US. Like any messy relationship, my status with home buying is: It's complicated.

On top of these pros and cons of contemporary homeownership, we're living in a settler-colonial state in the first place, benefiting from stolen indigenous land based on Western ideals of property rights. I promise I won't lead you down the rabbit hole of Anglo property law principles. But there are other possibilities for housing and our relationship with land and property, beyond the limited framework—either insecure tenancy or the speculative, for-profit housing market—that we've been offered.

Housing should be a human right, but in our current capitalist society, it's treated as a commodity, and millions of people currently face eviction in the richest country in the world.

So what's the moral of the story here? Everything sucks a little . . . for now. The world that I personally would like to live in offers options: you can access public housing that's super affordable, you can own a home if that's your thing (but without the expectation that you can amass immense wealth from it that would hurt a lot of other people), or you can rent some other form of affordable housing on land that's managed and owned communally.

And here's some good news: these examples exist in real life. We may not be destined to be serfs on an oligarch's land after all!!

AS SEEN ON
TV

Vienna, Singapore

PUBLIC HOUSING

STRUCTURE:

Government agencies fund the construction and maintenance of public housing units. Units may be rented or, in some places, owned through a long-term leasehold system.

BENEFITS:

- Federal government is large enough to pay for the massive investment needed to serve millions of families.
- Maintains housing affordability
- Mitigates homelessness

CHALLENGES:

- Securing the land to develop public housing could be detrimental to some communities due to "slum clearance."
- Little political will in the US from either Democrats or Republicans to invest in existing public housing or construct new units. (We know Congress hates to do literally anything.)
- Stereotypes and stigma about public housing among voters would likely deter their construction. Because NIMBYism.

Vermont, California, Massachusetts

COMMUNITY LAND TRUSTS

STRUCTURE:

Land is owned by a nonprofit, and its board decides how the land is developed. If housing is constructed, the nonprofit allows residents to enter a 99-year lease. Residents own their home, similar to a state-run leasing system. If a resident chooses to sell, the selling price must remain affordable.

BENEFITS:

- Can preserve affordability and mitigate displacement
- Decisions about the management of the land are done collectively, and the board includes residents.
- Targeted to low-and-moderate income families who may otherwise be unable to find secure housing in the rental market

CHALLENGES:

- Some of the more intangible benefits, like the sense of community, are not guaranteed
- The legal infrastructure to create them on a large scale isn't fully developed in many states
- Land in larger cities may be cost-prohibitive for nonprofits.

AS SEEN ON
TV

New York City

LIMITED EQUITY HOUSING COOPERATIVES

STRUCTURE:

Residents each own a share in the stock of their cooperative and pay a monthly membership fee to cover common expenses such as maintenance and reserves. Residents can vote on how the building is managed and governed.

BENEFITS:

- Intended to preserve affordability, as there are income limits to qualify for membership and reselling is restricted.

CHALLENGES:

- Can vote to privatize, allowing individuals to eventually put their home on the private real estate market, which could eliminate affordability. *

*NOTE: But there are some deterrents to privatization. In 2021, for the Mitchell-Lama co-op program, New York State passed a law that requires that 80 percent of residents vote on opting out of the program to privatize their development. If a vote to opt out fails, it places a five-year moratorium on a new vote.

brb, moving to singapore

While none of the previous examples are orthodox socialist solutions per se, they are examples of helpful reforms that exist in capitalist countries that can even the playing field. In Singapore, over 80 percent of its residents live in public housing flats. While the flats are developed and managed by the government, 90 percent of public housing residents own their home through a ninety-nine-year leasehold system. They can renovate, rent, and sell their flat and can keep the profits of any transactions, though there are rules to prevent investors from buying up the housing stock purely to flip it and earn a profit (like a five-year occupancy requirement). I don't know about you, but I'd take this any day over haggling with either a mortgage company or my landlord, who wants to hike my monthly rent up by $500 in one year because a Whole Foods is getting built down the block.

Unlike Federal Housing Administration loans and other government financing programs in the US, in Singapore the state-subsidized housing doesn't become private property that can be owned indefinitely. After ninety-nine years, the leaseholders must relinquish their property to the state to be leased to another family, and the government provides other housing for elders who may outlive the lease term. Singapore's long-term leases are also intended to maintain affordability. "Buyers would need to use less than a quarter of their monthly household income to pay for the mortgage installment of their first flat, a figure lower than the international benchmarks for affordable housing," according to Singapore's Housing and Development Board.

If you don't think these public, government-regulated options can work for us in the United States—we're a bigger country, you say, and like, so libertarian—then just look at our for-profit housing market and tell me you don't want to at least try.

fatal attraction—our addiction to property ownership is a killer!

As most of us have realized by one look at apartment listings (or when trying to buy a home), median wages since 1997 have grown way more slowly than rents and the cost of buying a home.

Remember that in Singapore you can own a home by paying less than 25 percent of your income on a mortgage through the government's long-term lease system. In the US, many tenants pay much more than that just to rent, largely because property owners are encouraged to get as much value out of their land as possible and most of us aren't getting paid enough.

RENT BURDEN IN THE U.S.

(2017)

48 percent of renter households in the U.S. are considered rent burdened. That means they pay more than 30 percent of their household income on rent. It's even worse for lower-income renters, where the rent burden is:

54%

for low-income renters

83%

for very low-income renters

89%

for extremely low-income renters

Clearly, a main theme of this book is "things are costing more and we're getting paid less!!!" Being paid less affects so many of the ways in which we live, including *where* and *how* we live. But, of course, capitalists' profits are growing just fine.

If you want to stir up your class rage a little more, I can tell you that "super-luxury" home sales have surged over the past few years, growing 35 percent from 2020 to 2021. "Super-luxury" is not that $3-million dream house you've had on your vision board for the past five years that has long since been snatched up. We're talking homes that sold for over $50 million.

In 2021, Jonathan Miller, CEO of appraising firm Miller Samuel, told Bloomberg, "Since 2014, there's been the establishment of a new class of property," referring to homes sold at $100 million or more. "Initially, it seemed comical or whimsical; these numbers we were seeing came across as a flash in the pan. But now we're in our seventh year of it."

Meanwhile, homelessness in the US has increased every year since 2016, and the rate of eviction filings is higher than in any other country studied by the Organisation for Economic Co-operation and Development (OECD). Marxists talk about carving up mansions and housing the homeless in them . . . and that isn't sounding so bad, right about now.

With housing considered as an investment, instead of primarily as a means of shelter, investor buyers are snatching up homes everywhere.

WAGES

EVICTIONS

INVESTOR PROPERTIES

GOOD VIBES

As data firm CoreLogic reported, investors made 27 percent of all single-family home purchases from January through September 2021, in the middle of the pandemic. This was up from about 16 percent at the same time in 2019. Who wants to bet activist and author Naomi Klein is penning her next chapter on disaster capitalism in real estate?

Investors are, of course, focusing on low-priced homes, hurting the chances of younger generations looking to make their first purchase. As the *New York Times* reported, as of May 2021, 93 percent of homes purchased by corporations were bought for under $300,000.

This trend has hit some predominantly Black neighborhoods especially hard. According to a *Washington Post* analysis of 2021 data in forty major metropolitan areas, "30 percent of home sales in majority Black neighborhoods were to investors, compared with 12 percent in other Zip codes." In my hometown of metro Atlanta—in Black communities where I attended church, tutored, celebrated Black college homecomings, and grew into adulthood—investors are snatching up homes like bandits. They're not there to pour economic activity and life into the community, like most homeowners. Their focus is to profit, either through house flips or luring in renters.

Along with Charlotte, Atlanta ranked first in the country for investor-purchased homes during 2020–21. In numerous zip codes where the population is majority Black, investors made up more than 50 percent of the buyers in 2021.

Homeownership is depicted as a racial equalizer. But how can America bill homeownership as the path to parity when it remains inaccessible for so many people? The Black homeownership rate has reverted to where it was before the Civil Rights Act of 1968 (i.e., the Fair Housing Act) was signed into law. Fifty-five years later, white Americans continue to be the disproportionate beneficiaries of the housing market.

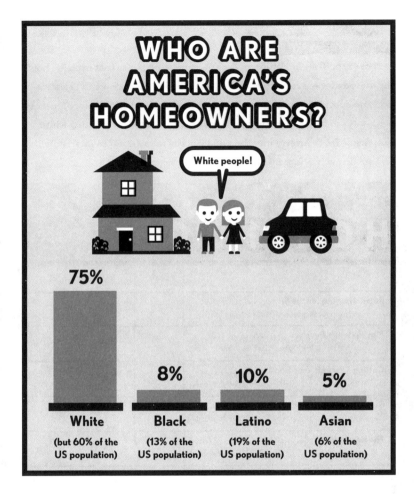

The racial homeownership gap isn't improving for millennials, either. According to a 2021 report from Apartment List, "White millennials maintain a homeownership rate that is substantially higher than non-white groups, and only barely lower than previous generations" of white families. God only knows what Gen Z is inheriting.

With rent becoming more unaffordable, cities are also seeing more people become unhoused.

There is endless literature on American housing policy that explains how we arrived at these racial disparities. Meanwhile, experiments in privatization and subsidizing developers have yet to create real affordability for most people. From New Deal housing programs that focused on uplifting white Americans from poverty into the middle class, to racial covenants, redlining, and subprime lending, there's a policy hit for every decade!

HOUSING
HOT 100

	Peak	Weeks on Chart
Public Housing for the Win . . . . Just Kidding Because We Segregate This, Too	1	4,576
Moving to the Burb . . . . The Highways feat. the White Flights	1	3,484
Cutting Through Your Hood . . . . The Feds feat. the Highways	2	3,484
Burbs for Me and Not for Thee . . . . Racial Covenant	3	5,044
The Red Line . . . . THOLC and Lender	2	4,420
Clear It Up . . . . Robert Moses	4	4,056
Defunding Everything . . . . Not the Police	1	3,000
Privatize . . . . DJ Private Equity (feat. HUD and the Neoliberals)	1	2,080
Equal Access . . . . Haha, It's Really Subprime Lending	3	936

A common takeaway from historical accounts of racial and wealth inequality is that policymakers should just increase access to the private home-ownership market. Not just to provide housing security, but to mitigate the racial wealth gap. But as researchers at the Samuel DuBois Cook Center on Social Equity point out:

> [T]he idea that homeownership creates wealth simply may put the relationship backward. Rather than homeownership creating wealth, having family wealth in the first place leads to homeownership, particularly high equity homeownership. . . . [B]lacks have minimal initial wealth to invest in homes or pass down to their children to assist with down payments, [and] without sufficient wealth in the first place, households have limited means to invest in homeownership. Wealth, after all, begets more wealth.

For renters and buyers, housing policy at all levels of government focuses on simply increasing supply because the "free market" (which we have never actually had in America, don't let anyone tell you otherwise!) leaves everything to supply and demand. When there is less money to be made renting to poor, low-income, and working-class people, what is a developer's incentive to increase supply for them? The government supplies some monetary incentives (like low-income-housing tax credits), but they clearly are not enough to keep masses of renters housed affordably and comfortably.

Policymakers also tend to ignore the fact that plenty of vacant houses are just sitting around. Don't worry, it's not because all these houses are abandoned. Some people just need to have their city house and their country house, oh, and their summer house and their winter house, too. And we can't forget some of the money-laundering high-rises, the Tinder Swindlers of real estate. These superwealthy homeowners can't fathom being taxed more for this luxury (nor can the industry that is built around their business).

Fundamentally, housing is a mess for millions of people because capitalist logic is a mess. And this logic just happens to align quite well with . . . (drum roll, please) . . . the Vicious Cycle of Why We Don't Have Nice Things. And so we have a fundamentally discriminatory system that encourages people to do whatever they can to keep their home value high (even if it means more discrimination), locking out a lot of other people from owning a home either because of race, class, or both.

Clearly we have our work cut out for us.

Solving the housing problem is tricky, and I won't even pretend I can answer it all in this chapter. For starters, unlike the workplace, where there are often clear class differences between multimillionaire or billionaire owners and their workers, you don't have to be anywhere close to a capitalist boss to be a homeowner. Because of that, homeowners are not an acute minority. Over the past decade, they've been about 65 percent of the US population, and they have fundamental interests that compete with renters.

Renters want to maintain affordability and housing security. Homeowners (and those who may have owner-occupied rentals) want the value of their homes and land to appreciate and to have the ability to evict tenants if they fail to pay rent.

We socialists are always looking to find common ground and solidarity.

finding love in a hopeless place

The super high-level answer to finding solutions for this complicated situation is that with a socialist alternative to capitalism, our underlying housing problems in the US—of millions of people facing low, stagnant wages and being unable to afford to live where and how they want—might no longer exist.

And under socialism, people could actually have the choice and freedom to live in whatever kind of home they want. Y'know, the things capitalists say we already have.

THE VICIOUS CYCLE OF WHY WE DON'T HAVE NICE THINGS

(Housing Edition)

Developers and banks want as much wealth as possible.

Our government at every level pushes for homeownership...and racist laws that restrict Black people from being homeowners.

Our housing market relies on property values rising.

White homeowners get told Black neighbors drive down their home value.

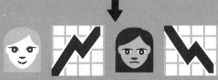

Values go up, affordability goes down, and the racial wealth gap persists.

Moms 4 Housing

Another way some people have addressed the issue is through straight-up resistance. In 2019, a group of women in Oakland, known as Moms 4 Housing, occupied a vacant house owned by corporate landlord Wedgewood Properties. The women were all unhoused mothers who were both protesting a serious issue and meeting a personal, practical need. Think of them like Rosa Parks for the twenty-first century. Yes, they were resistant about moving because they didn't have their own home, but they were also very intentional about making a larger point while being super relatable (I mean, moms! Who can be mad at moms??).

"This is a new face of homelessness, people that are working more than one job to hold it down," shared a Moms 4 Housing founder Sameerah Karim in a 2019 video interview. "[People] that are educated. That are in the process of getting their education. And it's no crime on our part. The crime is a society where we even have to be homeless."

Another homeless mother in the organization, Dominque Walker, was saddled with student loan debt. Confronted with an increasingly costly city, she struggled to find a permanent home and eventually found Karim. They banded together after finding out that Oakland was full of vacant homes and chose a house in West Oakland to occupy.

After their months-long protest gained national attention, Wedgewood was pressured to sell the home to a community land trust, OakCLT. OakCLT in turn rehabilitated the home, which Moms 4 Housing is now operating as transitional housing for other mothers and their children.

This local, DIY resistance invokes the spirit of another Oakland-born group: the Black Panther Party. Both organized around very personal, tangible problems in their community. The Panthers, for instance, got started in 1967 by helping kids cross the street to school after the city was slow to install a stoplight. And these grassroots movements can grow to address larger, systemic problems.

For Moms 4 Housing, this has been the vast commodification of housing. "Before we found each other, we felt alone in this struggle," their website reads. "We are coming together with the ultimate goal of reclaiming housing for the community from speculators and profiteers."

With this relatively small, but impactful, act of resistance, the women have already helped some families find stability and safety and encouraged a much bigger conversation around alternatives to our capitalist housing model, well beyond Oakland's borders. A mass movement of occupying vacant homes may not be the most practical, but never discount the effectiveness of just embarrassing these capitalists.

Figuring out how to scale up these local solutions to major enduring problems—without resorting to abstraction ("we just need a revolution!!!")—takes work. ✊🏽

Getting American capitalists (and people who think they're capitalists) to agree on anything that seems to marginally challenge the free market system—even just by giving people an option for an alternative—is a tall order. That's how absurd capitalism is here.

And let's be real. It's a bit daunting for a lot of us regular working people in the US, too. The thought of not owning a single-family house goes against what we've been taught our whole lives: that buying our own home is the American dream. I mean, millennials grew up on MTV Cribs, dreaming of Mariah Carey's Tribeca penthouse, and yet so many of us can't afford anything of our own. Of course we want to be able to give tours of our house and tell a stranger "this is where the magic happens."

Cooperatives and public housing come with hefty political challenges in the US and they're not perfect alternatives, which I've pointed out. Shoot, window-house-shopping on Zillow has become a hobby of mine, because I know homeownership can have its benefits.

But I'm also aware that private homeownership is not a panacea for community-wide social problems. It's a way, potentially, of having a reprieve from them. And as discussed, sometimes it reproduces and perpetuates those problems.

If we're going to be in a relationship with an economic system, does it have to be one that gives us such mixed results? Like with the image of mom-and-pop shops so often evoked to present capitalism as the ideal choice for hard-working, regular families instead of scary socialism (while multinational corporations laugh their way to the bank), we've been sold a particular version of the American housing dream. But the reality is less of a nineties rom-com with the perfect meet-cute and fairy-tale ending, and, again, more like the ups and downs of Nina and Darius in Love Jones. Fortunately, we don't need their grand gestures (at the last minute of the movie I might add!) to solve our housing crisis. We just need a steady commitment to try the many options that have worked in America in the past, and those that have been working outside of the US today. It doesn't have to be complicated, but it sure is "urgent like a motherf---er"! ✊

7
Capitalism's Twilight

"SHOW ME A CAPITALIST, AND
I'LL SHOW YOU A BLOODSUCKER"
—MALCOLM X

Energy vampires suck. In some relationships, we give and give, and the other person just wants to take and take from us. And if we ask for anything back, and they oblige occasionally, it's like they're doing us a huge favor. And of course they'll hold it over our heads forever.

In hypercapitalist USA, we give so much of our time and energy to our jobs. Meanwhile in the last several decades, our jobs have largely skirted any responsibility to pay us accordingly, while they suck the life out of us. Instead of stepping up, our government often looks the other way, and when we ask for support we get lectured about personal responsibility. Sometimes, if we're lucky, government leaders will reluctantly give us two crumbs to piece together (remember the COVID relief check drama from both parties?) or they make our lives even worse. But we're supposed to feel sooo grateful for those two crumbs.

So much of the cost of a basic social safety net—like affordable higher education and healthcare—are passed along to workers and consumers. And because we simply can't afford it, a lot of Americans are shouldering debt for those important things. And since these things are pretty necessary, a whole industry of lending has ballooned to *guarantee* that they'll profit from our desperation.

Welcome to the blood-sucking world of consumer finance, where big businesses (and elected officials in some cases) have forced millions

Why Are We Swiping Right on These Lending Bloodsuckers?

STUDENT LOAN VAMPIRE

ABOUT ME

- I will be with you forevvverrr. Can't get rid of me baby!
- My love for you will just grow and grow.
- I just have a lot of interest in you okay? I may stalk you and hound you for money, no matter where you move.

CREDIT CARD VAMPIRE

ABOUT ME

- I'll be with you wherever you turn looking for commitment. Yeah, I know we just met.
- I'll charge a lot for you to be with me. It's kind of criminal actually.
- You make one little mistake and I'll hold it against you for a really really long time.

JAIL VAMPIRE

ABOUT ME

- I have a thing for men of color. It's not a fetish, I promise . . . it's just a preference.
- If you can't pay me back, you'll barely see the light of day.

PAYDAY LOAN VAMPIRE

ABOUT ME

- I know your main chick isn't giving you what you deserve, so I'll help you out . . . but it'll cost ya.
- You can hit me up last minute when you're in a pinch, but of course I'll charge a premium. I know my worth!
- I'm kind of low-key, so I get away with a lot.

of us into indebtedness, from student loans and credit cards to payday lending and the criminal legal system. Yes, even our "justice" system has been caught up in the debt wave.

On top of wages that don't keep up with the cost of living, the increasing influence of the financial industry—in Congress, and in almost every aspect of our lives—has led to us having the most household debt ever in the United States.

It's easy to solely blame borrowers for making bad decisions. After all, your good ol' Uncle Larry was a "responsible adult" who went to a school he could afford, paid off his entire $7,000 college debt, and he would be livid if a president wiped out all the debt for other people (especially the colored ones).

With society's hyperfocus on borrowers, it seems like people largely ignore those who profit handsomely from our indebtedness.

This debt issue is not just about education. There's a whole crew of lending bloodsuckers trying to match with us. Swipe left!

not another teen debtor

Let's take a closer look at student loans. The way these vampires have crept into our lives—sometimes before we are legal adults—is scaryyy. Here are some horrifying numbers:

- Student loan debt is the second-highest category of personal debt after housing debt, totaling $1.59 trillion in the first quarter of 2022.
- The amount of student loan debt in the US is higher than the total wealth held by the entire bottom 50 percent of US households in 2018 ($1.54 trillion). Let that sink in a minute.
- Between 1995 and 2017, the balance of outstanding federal student loan debt increased more than sevenfold, from $187 billion to $1.4 trillion (in 2017 dollars).

- College education costs rose 103 percent since 1987. Median household income increased 14 percent.
- Race and gender make a difference too. Women hold nearly two-thirds of all student loan debt. Black men and women borrow more money to finance their undergraduate education than anyone else, and these numbers don't even include students who don't borrow any money at all.

something is *not right.*
(this, specifically, is not right.)

You've probably heard more about the hypothetical elite college students who will allegedly benefit from student loan cancellation than you have about the web of companies (and our own government agencies) profiting from our debt. Poor (okay maybe not *poor*) Yale grad Christine who spent summers in Nantucket and probably never needed a loan in her life is catching more heat than private companies like Maximus (the largest student loan company in the world), and other servicers who collect the money we borrow from the feds.

Literally as I type this, I'm staring down a pile of letters from companies still trying to take my money, under the guise of helping me pay off or postpone paying off my debt. One from the finance company SoFi has writing on the envelope saying it will give me a WHOLE $100 if I refinance my student loans with them. These lenders are *everywhere*.

How did it get so bad?

I spoke to Raúl Carrillo—a debt expert and deputy director of Yale Law School's Law and Political Economy Project—to find some answers. We're about to get into it.

DEBT

Q: What do you see is the problem with focusing the blame on students for student loan debt?

A: Higher education doesn't need to be a debt issue at all. California had public colleges that were free. Up until the 1960s, CUNY [City University of New York, New York City's public college system] had a relatively free system. The complicating factor here often became race and the idea that certain ideologies were being reproduced in colleges. That was Reagan's whole deal, you know, "they're training hippies and Black Panthers at Berkeley, so shut it down."

So conservatives make this an issue of "desserts," and liberals keep it as an issue of individual merit; both exclude the possibility of treating education for what it is: something that would benefit us all and is necessary for the reproduction of society.

Q: It's interesting you bring up the race issue, because I hear from elders, "I went to CUNY, and I paid like $2 a month." So you're talking about this propaganda and policy against truly making college super accessible. Yet, now it's almost a requirement to take out a loan to afford most good schools and it's sold as *the* key to success for young people of color. Do you think there's any correlation, given that this was happening at the same time?

A: I'm not going to speak for all people of color. But I know that in my community, certainly, it is absolutely held up that way as the thing that everybody needs to do. For this older generation, education became this narrative that if we have enough of those peak people, people with the right sort of papers, then things would be better for everybody.

And many community leaders stopped organizing, which won the rights for education in the first place. It has almost replaced the idea that we would fight for public goods in that way, at least that's how I think it's operating. We have this system where people in particular communities still believe that they have to [have an expensive degree] to get by, much less to build wealth, and that's an environment for exploitation. And that's when we get for-profit colleges taking it to the next level, and the debt just gets worse and worse. And that goes for public and private debt.

Q. So going into more of the logistics of how this works: Who actually owns our student loan debt?

A. It depends on what kind of a loan you have. For most of us, it is on the books of the Department of Education, which is to say, the federal government that prints the damn money in the first place. Nothing is hinging on your monthly payments. The Department of Education is not going to go insolvent. It is not a thing that is going to happen.

Yet they have this sort of revenue mindset, and that they have to be cost effective, even though they're loans and not expenses. It's a whole ecosystem of profiteering.

The government doesn't have to do things this way. But in the neoliberal era, this is the submerged state, right? It's behind all these private-sector companies. When you're talking about a debt to the government, you're essentially saying that certain people should have a tax or a penalty for coming up when the federal government doesn't even really need that money.

Q: So that leads me to my next question. Is it really that hard to forgive?

A. It is not. The executive authority is certainly there. My friend Luke Carian, who essentially wrote the core idea that [Elizabeth] Warren is using, proposes that we have a whole higher education system overhaul. It could be a more streamlined financing system, it could also just be grant-based rather than loan-based. In Australia, [the government] provides grants, and then they may or may not collect based on your income in the end, but it's not a creditor-debtor relationship. And it's not punitive.

But the government could cancel [student debt] now, pretty much indiscriminately, and it would have a progressive impact. We know that people in particular situations are forced to carry more debt, and the racial and demographic factors for that break down pretty much exactly as you'd expect them to. Thirty thousand dollars means the world to a working-class person.

Q: What are some socialist solutions to this problem? Other than, you know, ending capitalism tomorrow. What kind of reforms would be socialist reforms in the interim?

A. We have to get after the education system itself and the way it's set up financially. As long as the whole thing runs on localized property taxes [meaning wealthy neighborhoods have better public school funding], we have a huge problem. And the courts aren't going to let us relitigate that. So it's got to be through organizing. I don't think we get there any other way, and it probably starts at municipal, county, school district levels. But that's where socialism popped up in the United States originally anyway, right? ✊

While state governments used to invest in higher education, they've now passed that responsibility on to private companies who lend us the money. It's how neoliberal capitalism works in general: fundamental goods and services that the government should or could provide—affordable housing, education, healthcare, and utilities, for instance—are passed off to the private sector, which is more focused on their market share and motivated by profits than on providing quality, affordable services. Meanwhile, we get government cuts (i.e., austerity measures) to those services, and advocates have to lobby constantly to keep them off the chopping block.

This is super evident with higher education: there is a direct relationship between what states had historically been investing in public higher education and what public college and grad students owe to lenders. According to research, "If states had continued to support public higher education at the rate they had in 1980, they would have invested at least an additional $500 billion in their university systems. This amount is 'roughly equal to the outstanding student debt now held by those who enrolled in public colleges and universities.'"

oh my god we're back (here) again?

Let's talk about ABS. No, not the abs you want popping for your summer body (which is whatever body you happen to have in the summer, okay?). I mean Asset-Backed Securities.

An asset-backed security is a type of investment that makes money from some underlying asset-generating money. There's been a market for student loan asset-backed securities (SLABS) for a couple decades now. SLABS are investments based on revenue that comes from us paying back our student loans with interest. Our student loans get packaged into a security and student loan lenders sell these SLABS to buyers on Wall Street. If this sounds familiar, it's because Wall Street and lenders did similar finagling before the 2008 financial crisis, with home mortgages. And luckily the movie *The Big Short* actually kind of explained how it worked.

As with home loans in the wake of the 2008 financial crisis, there should be a lot more scrutiny on the greed of schools and lending institutions that push these products and the investors who profit from them.

As Raúl Carrillo reported in *Rolling Stone*, "Lenders, servicers, collectors and investors prosper while students suffer because schools increasingly rely on private tuition rather than public funding." Which means more borrowing to afford that tuition. That SoFi Super Bowl stadium won't pay for itself!

Basically, a lot of people in the private sector are getting rich off students and graduates. For financial companies involved, their investment is low risk (because again, it all goes back to the government in the end), but they get high rewards—they can charge any interest rate they want, while federal law keeps debtors on the hook for their loans even if they go bankrupt.

the debt is everywhere

Americans are relying on debt for other basic needs outside of education, using consumer credit cards and payday lending to close the gap between our stagnant wages and our rising cost of living. Because payday lending is particularly egregious, let's focus on this horrific bloodsucker. We could call payday loans the "James" (see Cam Gigandet's character in *Twilight*) of capitalist structures.

- Payday loans are "short-term high-interest cash loans made against borrowers' paychecks." And when I say high, I mean higher than Colorado on 4/20.

- Payday lenders charge about $15 in fees for every $100 they lend over a two-week period. This would convert to an APR of **391%**.

- Compare this to the average APR for credit cards, which was 16.45% in 2021.

Payday lenders are the biggest users and, unsurprisingly, Black people disproportionately rely on them. Like the subprime mortgages that were targeted to people of color (even to higher income households), payday lending is what some researchers call a form of predatory inclusion. Certain people, primarily Blacks and Latinos, are excluded from conventional credit markets but targeted for really, really shitty ones that have high interest rates. This "inclusion" (real hard air quotes here) builds on historical and contemporary racial exclusion.

As researcher Raphael Charron-Chenier found, "In 2016, nearly half of the households who used payday loans were nonwhite (47 percent), and black households in particular were 2.5 times more likely than white households to have used a payday loan."

You know how the right wing uses phrases like "right to work" when talking about laws that actually lower labor protections for workers? The narrative around "inclusion and access" often means predatory loan terms for Blacks and Latinos, from housing to education. It begs the question, what exactly are we "accessing"?

As big a problem as debt has become, it's just a part of an even larger capitalist phenomenon: the financialization of the US economy.

What's financialization? It just means that the financial sector—banks, lenders, hedge funds, the stock market, and other institutions that make transactions in financial products such as checking and savings accounts, investments, loans, and insurance, to name only a few—are taking up a larger share of the economy, as compared to industries like manufacturing, for example. These are the entities who benefit from all of this debt we're carrying.

This increased hoarding of wealth and political power obviously flows to the wealthiest people. So our economy overall is becoming less connected to everyday workers who produce real things or serve the average person. Meanwhile, incomes and wealth are distributed more and more to shareholders and finance professionals.

carceral credit

The criminal legal system is another lending vampire—and not even the hot, sparkly kind—but the energy sucking isn't just coming from the private sector. It's mostly facilitated by the government.

From the time someone gets arrested and goes to jail, to when they may be convicted of a crime and face time in prison, to when they are released, they're on the hook to pay someone money. On top of that, the work hours lost while in jail and the inability to pay for existing obligations—rent or a mortgage, for instance—while being locked up puts people further behind financially.

Advocates, like those behind Debt Collective, call this carceral debt. As organizer Manny Galindo says, carceral debt consists of "all forms of debt either created or worsened by an individual's involvement in the criminal legal system, from initial booking all the way to the end of reentry."

Bail Bond Basics

Bail bond companies charge a nonrefundable fee (usually about 10–15 percent of the bail amount).

You may have to sign a contract with the bond company allowing the company to take something significant of yours (your house, for instance) if you don't make your court appearances. That's your collateral.

If you don't show up for trial, the bail company will pay the court the full bail and then can take what you put up for collateral.

A key part of the debt problem starts with being jailed. Most people in jail have not been convicted of any crime. When people are arrested, in most places the only way they can be released from jail before their trial is if they pay a court-determined amount of money (bail), unless they're suspected of something really bad and bail isn't even offered. For felonies, the median bail amount is about $10,000. If you show up to all your court appearances, that bail money you pay the court gets refunded to you.

But wait, is that Uncle Larry whispering in your ear that most of us aren't criminals, so that's not our concern? Well, remember, people who go to jail haven't been found guilty of a crime. And it's not like police officers target certain communities and certain races of men who "fit the description" and lock them up arbitrarily or anything, right?

So anyway, most of us don't have $10,000 lying around to pay the court. That's where commercial bail bonds come in. Mind you, the US is one of only two countries in the world where a commercial bail system even exists. Look at us being exceptional again!

- **In 1990, by some estimates, 23 percent of people released before trial used a commercial bail bond. In 2009, that figure more than doubled to 49 percent.**
- **In 2019, about $15 billion in bail bonds were underwritten.**
- **The industry—backed by a small network of insurers—is estimated to collect as much as $2.4 billion in profit annually.**

The racial implications of this are daunting, and not just for the Black and Latino men who are disproportionately burdened by the monetary bail system. This financial burden falls heavily on low-income women, since they're often the people relied on to bail out male arrestees. As public defender Chanta Parker has said, "I can't tell you how many times I've been told to call the woman in the family. The mother, the grandmother, the girlfriend, the wife, the sister . . . to try and see if they could get the bail together. Probably 90 percent of the time, I was given the name of a woman to call."

Like any other corporate lobby (which we'll get into in Chapters 8 and 9), the companies behind bail bonds have been working furiously to keep lining their pockets. It's an industry that "maximizes profits at the expense of safety and justice," and they fight hard to stay relevant.

While other industrial countries have much lower rates of incarceration, and you may barely notice a police presence on a day-to-day basis, American racism and capitalism have completely warped our mindset. We've practically become immune to overpolicing and substantial incarceration. We've been convinced that these are necessary parts of our society. The racist criminalizing of Blacks and Latinos lines the pockets of big businesses, the financial underinvestment in many communities of color and ongoing wealth and income gaps make some kinds of crime more likely, and the rabid fearmongering around crime waves (especially during election seasons) fuels conservative, largely white voters to keep the system going. Meanwhile, policing and incarceration harms a lot of white people, too. It's a self-fulfilling prophecy.

Unlike students hounded by debt or workers who lose jobs, there's even more backlash against advocating for those who are incarcerated, because of the moralizing around crime. People with criminal records, regardless of the crime or conviction, get written off as undeserving of a second chance or even a chance to earn a basic livelihood.

Life is getting sucked out of so many of us, but the real villains just keep getting away with it. I probably speak for a lot of socialists when I say we feel like Regina Hall in *Scary Movie*. We're just out here yelling obnoxiously at the screen to warn people about the killer around the corner, but they keep walking right into the death trap.

If this all seems grotesque and dire and hopeless, well you'd be right about the first two. But some socialists aren't just yelling into the void while the horror unfolds; they've put their boots on the ground to organize.

With more people becoming indebted to capitalist bloodsuckers than ever before—and with the number of unionized workers shrinking—

nonprofits like Debt Collective have found a new opportunity to empower working-class people by unifying those of us who are in debt. Debt Collective is a debtor's union, where members pay a small amount in monthly dues, and these dues are used to help the union abolish and re-negotiate debt, give members tools to dispute their own debts, and fight for broader policies to abolish debt on a larger scale.

Socialist Astra Taylor, a cofounder of the Debt Collective, had just fin-ished preparing some student loan debtors for press appearances when we spoke on a late spring day in 2022. The union organized for months to demand that President Biden return to his campaign promise and abolish $10,000 of student loans for borrowers; he ultimately announced widespread debt cancellation a few months later. Debt Collective also organized debt strikes that preceded the Department of Education's abolition of over $10 billion in debt for students who enrolled in ITT and Corinthian, two private, for-profit schools that had been charged with unethical practices.

"How can we reframe debt from an issue of isolation and shame to a platform for collective action and political mobilization?"

– Astra Taylor

In conjunction with organizing work, they examined the president's legal authority and found that debt cancellation was within Biden's power. Then they put pressure on his administration to use it.

CANCEL STUDENT DEBT!

"Because of centuries-long war on workers, not everyone who is fully employed will get a chance to join a labor union," Taylor says. She sees a debtor's union as a "productive supplement," not a replacement of existing labor organizing, since the workplace is ultimately where the fight against capitalism and toward a socialist economy plays out. "You're robbed first by your boss, and then you're robbed by the creditor, who you're forced to engage with because you're underpaid. They're all connected to the deeper way our economy is structured." Taylor also offers some broader socialist solutions to the debt crisis. In addition to the abolition of unjust debts, she also agrees with Raúl Carrillo that education should be free and open to all. The "democratization of public goods is where we need to go. People shouldn't have to individually debt-finance the essentials of life."

"As socialists, we also need to think about finance more," she adds. "Obviously we want to strengthen labor unions. We would ultimately like to see some sort of workplace democracy and to shift the mode of production. But we also need to shift the modes of financing."

Taylor continues: "A capitalist economy is one in which markets dominate. There could still be markets for some things in a socialist society. But we don't need intermediaries that are profiting off our every exchange. And banking and finance right now are totally captured by private interests. So I think there's a lot to be said for making that infrastructure public."

Some socialists and progressives have been pushing the idea of postal banking for our everyday bank needs. Instead of paying large fees at check cashing places or facing exorbitant rates with payday lenders (both of which Taylor urges should be abolished) people with less access to traditional banks could go to the post office for financial services at lower rates. About a decade ago, our own US Postal Service published a white paper describing just how they could do it.

USPS already provides money orders (I've used them!), and when they published the report in 2014, they had about a 70 percent market share in the money order market. From 1911–1967, USPS also had a Postal Savings System that had billions of dollars in savings deposits. Since USPS is located all over the country, including low-income neighborhoods, it's already accessible to most people.

As an example of how they could keep people out of predatory transactions, USPS has proposed a "Postal Loan" program to provide small personal loans. Their research found that they could provide a $375 loan with only $48 in fees, versus the $520 in fees for the average payday loan. That's essentially an APR of 28 percent at the post office, versus 391 percent from a payday lender.

Granted, the USPS wasn't heralding postal banking as any kind of anti-capitalist model—it was largely proposed as a revenue generator. And of course they use the liberal messaging about "inclusion" for low-income households to show how postal banking can supplement our existing system. But it's a forward step, and it's roundly criticized by the banking industry and villainized by the right, so you know it's moving in the right direction.

Of course, under socialism the goal is for people's basic needs, which are frequently funded by credit cards and other loans, to already be met without the need to borrow money. Getting there—and making sure people aren't drowning in debt in the interim—will require ample strategizing and organizing. Joining a nonprofit that's already doing the work is one way to help.

In addition to Debt Collective, there's the New Economy Project. It's pushing for the city government in NYC to create its own public bank that isn't driven by a profit motive (which leads to those ridiculous interest rates that have us shackled like freaking debt slaves). Some groups, like the Modern Money Network, organize people to think differently about our economy and banking systems, as ways to "mobilize resources in support of the common good." MMN is full of lefty scholars who challenge traditional economics scholarship in the US that places primacy on the abstract "market."

"The real thorny, interesting questions are about strategy and tactics, and how do we actually build power in the here and now to even make people's lives marginally better," Taylor tells me, rhetorically. "I've just been on the phone with people for the last three days who were crushed by debt, suicidal. I don't think we need to have things be worse to suddenly be enlightened to have a revolution. No, we have to give people breathing room so we can survive and fight."

With more breathing room, more of us may be more inclined to fight, too. And it can have a real impact. As Taylor says, "when workers get organized and have power, debtors get organized and have power. Our strike, which began with fifteen people, grew to a few hundred. We just won six f&*king billion dollars of debt cancellation for 560,000 people," she says, referring to debt cancellation for students of the for-profit

Corinthian College that the group successfully advocated for. "And that was because we built a union, where people took this step of radical economic disobedience."

Despite what the movies tell us, we don't have to live on the proverbial edge, in a relationship with a sparkly, blood-sucking vampire who's very likely draining the life out of us—or definitely wants to—no matter how alluring their offer might appear. If the system allows predators to draw us into these traps, they will; it's in their nature.

But as in literally all rom-coms, there's always the hot friend disguised in a baggy graphic tee who's an actual good person just waiting for us to see the light. And we know how vampires hate the light. 🐾

8

Our Hearts Should Go On

"INHERENT IN CAPITALISM AND ESSENTIAL TO
ITS EXISTENCE ARE ABUNDANCE AND SCARCITY,
GROWTH AND NATURAL RESOURCE DEPLETION"
—**CAROLYN MERCHANT**

As we've learned, some people are perfectly fine watching you suffer while they reap the rewards of a relationship. When the (fictional) Titanic sank, Rose damn sure knew Jack could fit on that piece of wood she was floating on. The rich socialite splayed out in her lil' gown and watched the man she supposedly loved freeze to death instead of sharing her space. The Roses of the real world—wealthy, industrial countries—have been doing this to our Earth's natural resources since capitalism first emerged . . . and now they watch the world sink into the ocean. Literally.

Since capitalism's early development, we've been burning fossil fuels. The world, surprise, surprise, has been heating up faster and faster since the Industrial Revolution. Obviously, having a market of alternative energy isn't inherently socialist (Elon Musk, hello). But fossil fuel capitalism is the engine behind our climate catastrophe. It is fossil fuel capitalism that is preventing us from averting said catastrophe, and the damage is expensive as hell, if the whole *dooming little kids to a lifetime of health issues* isn't enough.

Around the globe, due to greenhouse gas emissions from fossil fuels, a hotter planet has led to extreme weather events like droughts, hurricanes, and heat waves. With drier conditions, "fires and floods are becoming more commonplace . . . sea levels are also rising, placing many low-lying communities, populous coastal cities and island states in jeopardy," the book *The Climate Crisis: South African and Global Democratic Eco-Socialist Alternatives* points out.

And like communities of color in the US who face the brunt of environmental injustice and the effects of fossil fuel capitalism, developing countries of the global South (mostly African and island states) are "most vulnerable to climate change but have contributed little to its genesis," wrote a team of researchers in 2016.

Scientists agree that our global temperature shouldn't be any higher than 1.5°C above what it was before industrialization. But we're on track to surpass that, and just a half degree above this 1.5°C increase in temperature will change things substantially, with more heat-related deaths and more diseases.

And there are other costs of burning fossil fuels. According to some research, air pollution causes 50,000 deaths and $445 billion in economic damage annually in the US alone. The US can save $3.5 trillion and avoid 400,000 deaths from air pollution by 2050 by switching to cleaner energy.

"To prevent further ecological destruction and have a chance to reduce the now decades-long climate chaos, capitalism has to go."

— *The Routledge Handbook on Ecosocialism*

The urgency of human-made climate change often leads us to focus on the fossil fuel industry, but the real issue is just capitalism, because it's also harming the planet in other ways. "Much of the historical and ongoing damage from capitalism, like species extinctions, world deforestation, lead contamination, and radioactive waste, is either entirely irreversible or irreversible relative to multiple human lifespans," warn the editors of *The Routledge Handbook on Ecosocialism*. THIS IS FINE!!

But none of this is groundbreaking information if you've turned on a TV at all in the last twenty years. It's often just too depressing to think about because we feel like we don't have any control over the state of the world, other than buying those goofy paper straws hoping they save a turtle. Or we boycott having kids, as if debt didn't already delay parenthood enough. And really, it's not that most of us reading this need to be convinced of anything. We're being held hostage by a tiny minority of fossil fuel capitalists, the banks that invest in them, and the politicians who benefit from downplaying climate change. The key, then, is what do we do about it?

There is a glimmer of hope. But before we get to that, let's take a close look at the lengths to which these capitalists and their cronies go so that they can maintain their power and profits while the planet burns. Instead of resignation and disappointment, maybe it'll light a fire under our a$$ (too soon?) to fight back.

pretty little liars

It's not a good look for fossil fuel companies to continue denying climate change. Instead, big oil and gas companies have engaged in PR campaigns touting their commitment to clean energy (aka "greenwashing") on one hand while reportedly doing relatively little to shift their business strategies toward alternative energy. Remember how Cal, Rose's grimy rich fiancé in *Titanic*, lied and said that he would save Jack from a sinking ship? It wouldn't be effective for Cal to be antagonistic, so he played nice to get what he wanted. And that's how these companies play in our faces about our planet. They make us expect one thing, but the reality is quite another.

THE MATH ISN'T MATHING

More innovation & technology		Cleaner energy		More oil refineries and pipelines ???

. . . but that's an equation that the industry and the politicians in their pockets seem to think people will believe.

In a study of major oil companies from 2009–2020—including Shell, Chevron, ExxonMobil, and BP—three researchers concluded that "the transition to clean energy business models is not occurring, since the magnitude of investments and actions does not match discourse. Until actions and investment behavior are brought into alignment with discourse, accusations of greenwashing appear well-founded."

Besides direct industry practices, fossil fuel companies are hiding behind lobbies that do the dirty work of averting any real transition to clean energy.

In early 2022, Mike Sommers, the former chief of staff for former Speaker of the House John Boehner, pinned a graphic to the top of his Twitter page. Titled "Taking Climate Action," it included several bullet points about how the government and industry can address the risks of climate change, including "accelerate technology and innovation" and "advance cleaner fuels."

Just below that tweet was a link to an interview with Sommers on Fox Business, where he emphatically stressed the need for "more refineries, more pipelines" and "more investment in the oil and gas sector in the United States. . . .We need to incentivize as much production as possible because that's the way we're going to get prices down for American consumers as much as possible," he told the anchor.

Amid a year of increased gas prices, inflation, and a war in Ukraine, Sommers homed in on a message that would keep his industry happy: Drill, baby, drill. Yes, while touting "climate action," he encouraged an increasing amount of oil and gas production.

Sommers was getting paid handsomely for this cognitive dissonance. After his time as Speaker Boehner's chief of staff, Sommers landed a job as president and CEO of the American Petroleum Institute (API), a lobby that represents US natural gas and oil production interests. According to the lobby's latest available 990 IRS return, in 2019 Sommers earned a hefty $3,000,000 in compensation from API.

API formed in 1919 to represent the oil industry after World War I, when petroleum needed to be deployed quickly to the armed forces. It now includes about 600 member organizations in oil and natural gas. Its origin story is replete with lofty rhetoric about its dominance in the US, asserting that "the industry is changing our country's narrative and altering its trajectory in historic terms." Yeah, our coastal cities being underwater would be historic all right.

The industry claims it can coexist with effective climate action, but API and other trade groups have been busy rigging the system (pun intended) to keep alternative energy industries from actually existing. And like the private healthcare sector, oil and gas lobbies have couched their business interests in hollow conservative tropes about so-called "choice" and "freedom."

This is what we call MONEY IN POLITICS.

The industry spent a crap-ton of money trying to convince the public that this was the only way. In a 2020 Facebook ad blitz, twenty-five advertisers produced 25,147 ads for the industry, according to data studied by the nonprofit watchdog InfluenceMap.

This ad campaign came just after then-presidential candidate Joe Biden unveiled his plan to increase clean energy. "This indicates the industry is now using social media to directly reach a vast audience and influence public opinions on climate change and the energy mix," InfluenceMap stated. Russian bots, but make them good ol' American oil barons.

Among the ads were conservative, patriotic messages like "Don't let radicals destroy our way of life!" (courtesy of New Mexico Oil & Gas) and a more sober message, "shutting down local oil and gas production would force us to increase reliance on unstable foreign oil," sponsored by Californians for Energy Independence, a nonprofit that's actually a coalition of various oil trade groups.

In just the beginning of 2021, the oil and gas industry and their trade associations spent over $55 million on lobbying, and much of this went to politicians. Public Citizen analyzed campaign finance data and found that the 29 members of Congress (all Republicans) who denounced the Biden administration's pause on new leases of public land and water for oil and gas drilling "received a combined $13.4 million over their careers from oil and gas interests."

Of course, politicians on both sides of the aisle have long been playing footsie with the big oil and gas (and sometimes coal) companies, using the rhetoric of energy independence from spooky foreigners to protect fossil fuel companies. Despite all the evidence presented before them from climate scientists, we're told there's nothing to worry about. Sounds like your average *gaslighter*.

When you hear this, chances are you're being gaslighted:

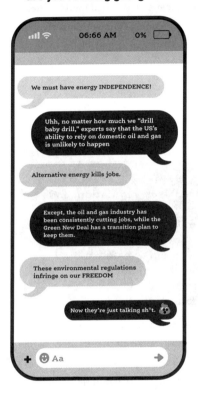

It also doesn't help that some unions in the oil and gas trades, whose workers are disproportionately white and male, have rejected laws that regulate the industry. In 2021, for example, a California union opposed a state law that would have prevented oil drilling near schools and communities (which tend to be Black and Latino), citing job losses.

And where would we be without the capitalists who run the world's largest banks and state-run financial institutions getting their grubby hands in all of this? According to the report *Banking on Climate Chaos 2022*, the world's sixty largest banks spent $4.6 trillion on fossil fuel investments since the 2015 Paris climate agreement. In 2021 alone, they spent about $742 billion to finance fossil fuels.

"Even in a year where net-zero commitments were all the rage," the 2022 report states, "the financial sector continued its business-as-usual driving of climate chaos. Fossil fuel financing plateaued last year, amid a lagging recovery from the COVID-19 pandemic—yet at levels still higher than in 2016, the first year after the Paris Agreement was adopted."

Plus, despite the rhetoric of lobbyists like Mike Sommers, who have used high gas prices to call for increasing oil production in the United

States, "the US can't drill its way to lower gasoline prices," environmental groups have warned. Since the US is fully integrated into the global market, an increase in crude prices globally means prices also increase here. It doesn't matter what percentage of the oil comes from within our own borders. As a coalition of environmental advocates urged, "[t]he answer to high gasoline prices is not to triple-down on a failed system," but rather a "separation of oil and state."

Neoliberal reform that keeps polluters from being directly regulated from the government also doesn't cut it. As Rhiana Gunn-Wright, the coarchitect of the Green New Deal, said:

> "Neoliberalism has ensured less regulation and more power for markets . . . [this] reinforces racial disparities such as Black-white wealth gaps, housing and school segregation, and, most acutely for frontline communities, disproportionate exposure to air pollution and other environmental harms."

While it feels like we're just biding time on a sinking ship, a group of socialists have been working to avoid a catastrophic glacier. Beyond weaning the world from fossil fuel extraction, they want to get us out of the grip of a capitalist system that has plundered the planet for generations.

open the door . . . to ecosocialism

Ecosocialism envisions a world where meeting everyone's basic needs is more important than corporations' profits, production of goods and services are democratically owned and managed, and those goods and services are produced with a "commitment to a safe climate." There are some steps we can achieve before we get to this.

A CYCLE OF HOW WE CAN HAVE NICE THINGS

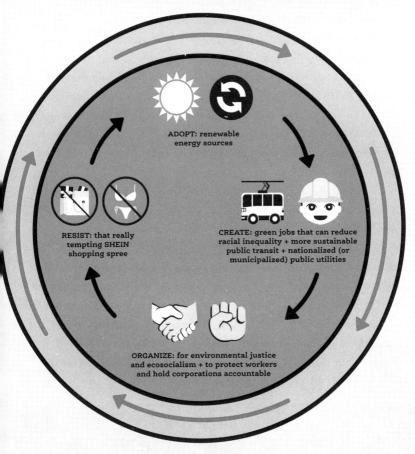

ADOPT: renewable energy sources

CREATE: green jobs that can reduce racial inequality + more sustainable public transit + nationalized (or municipalized) public utilities

ORGANIZE: for environmental justice and ecosocialism + to protect workers and hold corporations accountable

RESIST: that really tempting SHEIN shopping spree

= a greener planet where we can probably prevent impending doom

Conservatives like to hop on that part about curbing consumerism to threaten you with sCarY SoCiAlistS who want to snatch burgers and SUVs out of your hands. Of course, getting a new SHEIN wardrobe every season just to look cute for the 'gram is not in line with ecosocialism. Still, we can't just recycle, reduce, reuse, and personal-responsibility our way toward averting disaster. As scientist Michael Mann said, "focusing on individual choices around air travel and beef consumption heightens the risk of losing sight of the gorilla in the room: civilization's reliance on fossil fuels for energy and transport overall, which accounts for roughly two-thirds of global carbon emissions."

It's like rich dudes on the Titanic getting mad at the poor people in third class for using an ounce of fuel to turn the lights on in their rooms, while they're the ones directing the ship to sail faster toward disaster.

Ecosocialists, meanwhile, are ignoring the capitalists' orders. Ecosocialism is set apart from regular-degular socialism to reflect "a new understanding of capitalism as a system based not only on exploitation but also on destruction—the massive destruction of the conditions for life on the planet." As activist Michael Löwy points out, the socialism that developed in the twentieth century, like social democracy and Soviet-style communism, was, "at best, inattentive to the human impact on the environment and, at worst, outright dismissive."

A Whole
NEW W🌎RLD

with Thea Riofrancos

Q: People have these dire ideas about how the Earth is just ending and there's nothing we can do. What have you found is effective to encourage them?

A: There's just been such an evisceration of working-class political agency in the US by the destruction of unions and repression of the Black Power movement, and it's really laid the groundwork for people being demobilized and disconnected from politics.

I think it's critical for movements that want to reach a mass scale to focus on reaching ordinary people. Basically all of my activist work on these topics has been through the Democratic Socialists of America. My start was in local energy democracy work. Our goal was to actually have a public takeover of the privately owned monopoly utility company, National Grid. We had this ambitious goal that is the fullest sense of ecosocialism, this idea of public ownership in the energy sector.

We also had short-term goals. One was to really engage in popular education of National Grid's role in Rhode Island's energy sector. We would go out and canvass, set up tables at community events. When there were specific opportunities to really engage people in the policy process, we would turn out people to public hearings. We actually had influence, along with other groups that we were in coalition with, in reducing one of their proposed rate hikes.

Q: How do ecosocialists envision the labor movement divorcing itself from fossil fuel capitalism and embracing

alternative energy as a potential engine for jobs, especially when there are a number of workers in unionized labor employed by the oil industry?

A: I don't want to downplay that that is a really challenging topic. There are parts of the labor movement, or labor movement leadership, especially, that have been hostile to certain climate or renewable energy legislation or regulation because it would have a material impact on those industries. Those workers depend on those industries in the short term for their paycheck. That dependency, that vulnerability of those workers, is what also allows bosses to exploit those fears.

Ideally, labor union leadership in those sectors would be thinking more long term, like "what is gonna guarantee security?" What guarantees security for those workers is not tying them more to jobs in what hopefully is a dying fossil fuel industry. It's thinking about economic security that goes beyond fossil fuels.

I think that looks like fighting for a job guarantee, fighting for an *actual* just transition, and not just the rhetoric around retraining, but making sure there's real money on the table, that their members are going to be guaranteed their same wages and benefits as they transition to other parts of the energy sector that aren't tied to fossil fuels.

We need concrete campaigns for more legislation broadly, like the PRO Act [Protecting the Right to Organize Act of 2021], that would improve the bargaining power and material security of workers.

But to pivot, when we think about the working class more broadly, who is it? It's women, it's people of color, it's the service industry, it's health workers, it's education workers. And I think that the story changes a little bit in terms of organizing and engagement, and winning workers over to a kind of Green New Deal vision. It's different when you're doing outreach to a nurse—their job does not depend on the continuity of fossil fuels. And in fact, nurses and other health-care workers see the negative public health impacts of pollution all the time. They also tend to be more progressive. Their unions, in some cases, have made very progressive statements about climate change and about the Green New Deal.

The working class is complex, it's heterogenous, it's diverse, and there are different strategies for different types of workers in terms of building a working-class movement for climate justice.

Q: In an ecosocialist America, when you look outside, what do you envision?

A: For me, ecosocialism feels like more leisure time. That might not at all be the first thing that comes to mind when someone thinks the word socialism, but we're overworked and for the most part producing things that make a profit for capitalists that cause environmental harm. Whether we're talking about fast fashion or fast food, we produce these things as a society that are harmful to all of us.

The less we work, and the more we can shorten the working week and make sure that people don't have to work multiple jobs just to get by, the better things are for the environment. Working more as a society creates more emissions. We need energy to power all of that production.

A key part of socialism is having more time with family, friends, community; to spend outside in nature; or to spend in a library reading a book. There are all these activities that are not harmful for the environment that humans love doing, whether it's going to the theater, riding a bike, hanging out with our friends, cooking a great meal together, these are things that don't have a big environmental impact that are very rewarding and gratifying and that build community, which is important.

A second thing is having more forms of public recreation. Whether we're talking about bikes, or truly public and accessible beaches, or we're talking about national parks, hiking. It doesn't all have to be in nature. I'm including libraries in this or even thinking about our schools as being places where communities gather, having these public places that are free to everybody, to access and enjoy and that are oftentimes carbon neutral. They're places where you are communing with others, communing [with] nature, building relationships. You are not producing things that that need to be thrown out once they're done.

It's about creating a society in which we can democratically choose what we do and we are not constantly being harmed by pollution from fossil capitalism. And, again, we have that material security to live a different type of life than many Americans are subjected to. ✊🏽

Like we've discussed in other chapters, many progressive policies proposed in the US—from single-payer healthcare to student debt cancellation—are popular. Who doesn't want more leisure time? How many of us really want to spend forty hours or more a week literally fueling capitalism? The key is getting enough of us together to do something about it.

"We have to organize a strong independent base," socialist activist Kali Akuno, who we met in Chapter 3, told Jacobin in 2019. "Without that this epic issue will be held hostage to forces seeking to maintain the capitalist system as is, whether it be the Democratic or Republican variety of this worldview and its articulated interests. And we have to build this base to advance two strategies at once."

Getting a mass movement in the US to advocate specifically for ecosocialism will take some time. But we can take some baby steps to save ourselves before we get to the "freeze in the middle of the ocean and fight over lifeboats" part of the timeline.

Akuno and his colleague Joshua Dedmond, an activist born and raised in Jackson, Mississippi, are encouraging people in that Southern city to just look out for each other through mutual aid and cooperative economics. "There needs to be folks helping each other," Joshua Dedmond tells me. "These are immediate things that make folks ready to understand their placement in power and understand their placement in governance."

Dedmond and I spoke about a month after the Jackson water crisis made national news. The predominantly Black city was suffering from a lack of investment in its water infrastructure. The lack of clean running water was declared a national emergency. "It's really important that we showed up the way we did with the water crisis," Dedmond shares. Cooperation Jackson, a group Akuno cofounded, helped distribute water throughout the city to those who couldn't access it. "[We] meet people's immediate needs and then follow up with the high-level stuff, and [we] give them pieces and real strategic, thought-out political education. Be consistent and people will come around."

Cooperation Jackson aims to emulate the way that, in the 1970s, the Black Panthers provided services and met material needs of Black people in Oakland and mobilized them to act. The organization's goal is to form sustainable cooperatives that would serve Jackson residents, including with solar insulation/green retrofitting and waste management/recycling.

the earth should go on and on

Scientists have been trying to sound the alarm for generations. They have shown us convincingly that our world is burning up. They've spotted the glacier a long time ago, but lots of rich, powerful people want to see the *Titanic* continue its course, and some of them, like Cal, will lie about trying to save us. As long as there's money to be made, they'll keep trying to make it. But ecosocialists aren't trying to move up to a higher deck on a sinking ship and cosplay—and have flings with—the wealthy; they want us to steer ourselves toward the safety of a habitable planet.

A bunch of other nerds can write all the books, policy briefs, and news reports they want (me. I am nerds) stressing the urgency of this moment. But as with every other inch of progress we've managed in this world, mass movements are necessary. If capitalists and politicians are hogging up life rafts after sinking the ship, we will have to act to save ourselves. ✊

9

Strings Attached

> "THE CAPITALISTS OFTEN BOAST THAT THEIR CONSTITUTIONS
> GUARANTEE THE RIGHTS OF THE INDIVIDUAL, DEMOCRATIC
> LIBERTIES, AND THE INTERESTS OF ALL CITIZENS. BUT
> IN REALITY, ONLY THE BOURGEOISIE ENJOY THE RIGHTS
> RECORDED IN THESE CONSTITUTIONS."
> —HO CHI MINH

Big money in politics has become a huge, expensive problem. Like mixing money and romance, it usually doesn't end well. We saw it with the early healthcare debates and then with fossil fuel capitalism. The US talks a good game about democracy and the fundamental rights of voters, but even that is barely holding on. We have politicians backed by tons of cash who use cutesy phrases such as "choice," "freedom," "pro-life" and, y'know, "citizens united," to hide the fact that we're getting screwed, and not in a good way.

Wealthy political donors are like all those "benevolent" rich kids in rom-coms: they're doing the hapless, innocent kid a favor out of the goodness of their hearts, giving them a makeover and setting them up to be popular. But there are always strings attached—a law passed here, a tax break there—and in some cases the intentions might even be cruel.

cruel intentions

"Train for extreme violence," a Parler user wrote on the social media network in late November 2020. "I hope the day never comes but at least I know I'm ready to defend. Don't be helpless. Train as if your families safety depends on it. It's our ultimate responsibility as men.

#getready #apocalypse #civilwar #dontbeavictim #dontbeasheep #free-domfighters."

The post was accompanied by a picture of a man, presumably the post's author, posed in front of a Christmas tree and armed with an automatic rifle and a tactical vest with a bunch of other gun stuff.

This dire warning I saw wasn't a response to some imminent military invasion. It was a reaction to President Biden winning the 2020 election. Thousands of similar messages proliferated on Parler under the hashtag #CivilWar the same month Biden's victory was announced, with some more explicit pronouncements of "death to Democrats" and just casual photos of nooses peppering the network.

Social networks like Parler (which got off the ground thanks to Rebekah Mercer, the rich daughter of a hedge fund owner) weren't the only catalysts for the January 6 insurrection—it was billionaire donor money, too. Talk about rich kids with cruel intentions. Take Richard Uihlein—the cofounder of the Wisconsin-based Uline shipping supplies company—and his wife, Elizabeth, who have been quietly arming the right with an influx of cash in support of right-wing politicians and causes.

Among the groups that organized the "March to Save America" that stormed the Capitol were the Tea Party Patriots, which received $4.3 million in donations from the Ed Uihlein Family Foundation (a foundation named after Richard Uihlein's father) between 2016 and 2020. This group posted this announcement on the event's website:

> On January 6, 2021, millions of Americans will descend upon Washington DC to let the establishment know we will fight back against this fraudulent election.
>
> Take a stand with President Trump and the #StopTheSteal coalition and be at The Ellipse (President's Park) at 7am. The fate of our nation depends on it.

Though the January 6 insurrection was an extreme example, it was merely the outgrowth of long-standing practices in American politics: conservative politicians tap into the fears of the right (and increasingly of the far right), capitalists support those politicians, and we get public policy that benefits capitalists at the expense of the working class of all races. Why just focus on foreign interference in our elections when we have oligarchs like this right here at home?

And the web of their influence is about as messy as a Shonda Rhimes drama. While Richard Uihlein's family foundation funded fringe groups, his company's PAC (i.e., Political Action Committee—more on these beasts later) was the largest donor to Club for Growth Action in 2022, as it has been for the past four Congressional election cycles.

Club for Growth Action is "dedicated to a single mission: defeating big-government politicians and replacing them with pro-growth, limited government conservatives," according to its literal mission statement. In Republican-speak, that means pro-growth for the already wealthy and maximum government involvement to keep it that way.

This has funded the successful election campaigns of some of the most despicable Republican senators you can imagine.

It's one thing if all this money being thrown around ultimately served low-income Americans and the working class, y'know the whole trickle-down BS we've heard for decades. Instead—while lining their pockets with even fatter tax breaks and subsidies and curbing regulations on their riches—capitalist megadonors are enabling the erosion of public safety, infringing on reproductive rights, bulldozing the labor movement, and upending voting rights. They're fueling racial resentment, right-wing violence, and anti-LGBT bigotry. Even public K-12 schools are being threatened by billionaires who influence our politics.

AS THE WORLD BURNS

Club for Growth (CFG) ——— **Uline, Inc's PAC**
formed by billionaire Richard Uihlein, is the top funder of CFG

CFG's super PAC

#1 donor in various election cycles to senators:

Ted Cruz, R-TX

Ron Johnson, R-WI

Josh Hawley, R-MO

Rand Paul, R-KY

Rick Scott, R-FL

David Perdue, R-GA

From among one or more of these senators, we got proposals to:

1) Eliminate the federal minimum wage altogether. Let those pure, sweet markets decide!

2) Cut Medicare and Social Security.

3) Allow people to carry around guns with no permit . . . and offer the usual tHoUgHts aNd pRaYeRs when the inevitable happens.

the yassification of public education

Joining Richard Uihlein as a top donor to Club for Growth is billionaire Jeff Yass (ugh, nooo), an options trader with a $12 billion net worth. His company, Susquehanna Trading Partners, has been Club for Growth's second-highest funder, after Uline, since 2018.

Instead of focusing almost exclusively on Republican beneficiaries, however, Yass has also contributed to a smattering of Democrats in federal elections and to conservative Democrats in his home state of Pennsylvania. In that state, money has gone toward school privatization campaigns and opposing candidates who support teachers' unions—but it doesn't *appear* to come from Yass directly. It gets donated through his Students First PAC. With such an inspiring name, you'd never know that Yass, Pennsylvania's richest person, cofounded the PAC with two other Wall Street traders.

Yass has also directed money to the Commonwealth Children's Choice Fund, which had nearly $20 million in cash by the end of 2021. My review of its campaign finance report in 2021 shows that Yass's Students First PAC gave $12 million to the Children's Choice Fund that year. Our good friend Dick Uihlein contributed another $4.25 million. I guess it would be weird if they called it the "billionaires' choice fund," but it's pretty obvious who's choosing things here.

Like the Students First PAC, Commonwealth Children's Choice Fund is geared toward school privatization, and it directs money to Republicans in the Pennsylvania state legislature. Among them is Scott Martin, who sponsored a bill in 2021 proposing "the largest transfer of taxpayer dollars out of public schools" in the state's history.

So why does this matter?

As author Jim Freeman shared in the Oct. 2022 issue of *Current Affairs* magazine, capitalists "can take a $650 billion business, or $650 billion

THE VICIOUS CYCLE OF WHY WE DON'T HAVE NICE THINGS

PUBLIC SCHOOL EDITION

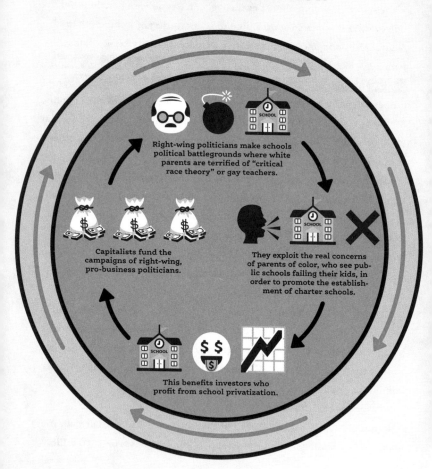

Right-wing politicians make schools political battlegrounds where white parents are terrified of "critical race theory" or gay teachers.

They exploit the real concerns of parents of color, who see public schools failing their kids, in order to promote the establishment of charter schools.

This benefits investors who profit from school privatization.

Capitalists fund the campaigns of right-wing, pro-business politicians.

industry, which is the public school industry, and transfer it from public to private hands. So when they do that they can profit directly. They can profit indirectly by controlling the agenda by using curriculum to better support their goals, which we've seen extensively in recent years."

In his book *Rich Because of Racism*, Freeman outlines the various ways the rich fatten their piggy banks through privatization. This includes "investing in real estate and leasing space to charter schools," "providing cleaning, food preparation, student transportation, security, accounting, legal, and consulting services to charter and private schools," and "producing the standardized tests that drive the school privatization agenda," among many other profit generators.

But most wouldn't view school privatization as racist—even if it may harm Black and brown kids the most—because capitalists often present charter schools as the antidote to public schools that leave children of color behind. For instance, in June 2022, the home page for the Commonwealth Children's Choice Fund had photos of just five people prominently featured, and three of these were Black kids. Every single sentence in their description had the word "opportunity" in it, as if the homepage was concocted in an AI social-justice word generator.

The attack on public K-12 schools is yet another example of the Vicious Cycle of Why We Don't Have Nice Things, with a bonus of pretending to be a universal good for young Black students.

Billionaire charter school proponents are like those serial monogamists who keep getting into relationships instead of working on themselves. They constantly find unwitting partners who are lured by their false promises, such as campaign ads that assure people that "small-government" politicians are their best choice and privatization is a big upgrade. Exploiting racist fears behind the scenes has long been key in keeping up the charade.

the willie horton formula

In the fall of 1988, the National Security PAC seized on an opportunity to sink the presidential campaign of Massachusetts governor and Democratic presidential nominee Michael Dukakis. Led by political consultant Floyd G. Brown and a handful of other conservatives who supported George H. W. Bush's campaign, NSPAC produced an ad linking Dukakis to a convicted murderer named Willie Horton.

In the ad, a picture of Horton—a Black man—flashed on screen. Horton committed a crime while he had a temporary "weekend pass" from a Massachusetts prison. NSPAC implied that the violence was due to Dukakis being soft on crime. The ad would symbolize the willingness of Republicans to unethically (and often misleadingly) stoke racial fears to win votes. Media from other conservative PACs followed, with similar messaging, leading up to the 1988 general election. The narrative stuck, and it worked.

Bush won the presidency. That year, Brown created a nonprofit called Citizens United. Citizens United went on to rake in millions of dollars, using this money to promote conservative media that has made a habit of fudging the truth to rile up the conservative base's fears.

Yes, one of the same men behind the infamous 1988 Willie Horton ad also eased the path for a minority of monied interests to pour billions of dollars into campaigns decades later, thwarting popular policies that could benefit most Americans for years to come.

BACKGROUND: Citizens United, a 501(c)(4) nonprofit corporation, funded a documentary against Hillary Clinton around the 2008 presidential elections. But federal law prohibited them from releasing it because it was funded by money Citizens United made in their regular course of business (i.e., from their "treasury") and was going to be released very close to an election; making it clear it was a form of illegal "electioneering." Citizens United lost their case in lower courts and ultimately appealed to the Supreme Court.

WHAT SCOTUS DECIDED: The court found in favor of Citizens United, deciding that these kinds of restrictions on corporations (which legally include nonprofits like Citizens United) violate the constitutional right to free speech, and upending over a hundred years of legal precedent prohibiting corporations from using their treasury for federal elections.

THE RESULT: Since *Citizens United*, large sums of money, notably from dark money groups, are increasingly pouring into campaigns, and a smaller number of rich bros (and some rich chicks) are contributing a larger share of campaign contributions. As NYU's Brennan Center for Justice tells us, "thanks to the Supreme Court's jurisprudence, a tiny sliver of Americans now wield more power than at any time since Watergate, while many of the rest seem to be disengaging from politics."

In 2012, 37 individual donors gave at least $2 million EACH to elections. By 2016, that number jumped to 110.

The 2016 election cycle cost just under $6.5 billion

A group of about 32,000 people gave over $2.3 billion (35% of the total)

Among those donors were a group of under 200 people. JUST 200 PEOPLE gave almost $1 billion combined.

To summarize, this is what money in politics looks like, and we haven't even touched on dark money or Super PACS yet. You're in for a real treat!

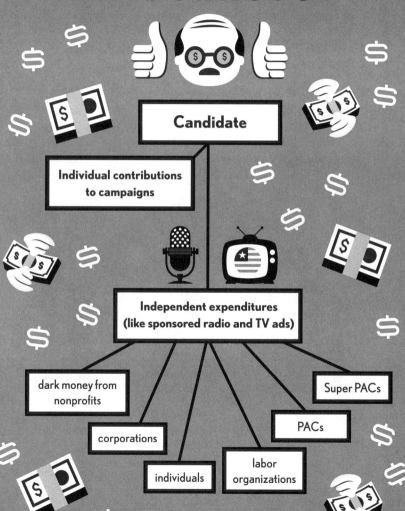

WTF Is Dark Money?

- **Money that is routed through nonprofits that aren't legally required to disclose their donors.**

- **The top groups behind dark money donations largely support conservative campaigns.**

- **$750 million in dark money went to the 2020 election. Nearly a quarter billion was for ads alone. This compares to only $1 million in 2006.**

PACS VS SUPER PACS

Super PACS cannot donate directly to federal candidates, but they can accept and spend unlimited amounts of money on their behalf for independent expenditures, like TV ads.

In 2020, according to campaign-finance tracking organization OpenSecrets, the top ten organizations and employees funding super PACs spent nearly $1 billion in the 2020 election cycle alone.

After lavishing political hopefuls with *Pretty Woman*-esque shopping sprees and fancy dates (okay, really just donations and some lobster dinners), of course capitalists want something in return. And for corporations that don't spend big bucks financing politicians and campaigns directly, they always have lobbying.

table for two

Companies are spending big bucks making sure that they have a seat at the legislative table and can get laws passed in their favor.

$119 Million: Oil & Gas

$121 MM: Business Assoc.

$153 MM: Insurance

$179 MM: Electronics Mfg & Equip

$357 MM: Pharmaceuticals/Health Products

2021

In 2022, **$3.77 BILLION** was spent lobbying Congress, with companies and trade organizations (like the National Association of Realtors) shelling out the most money to persuade the federal government to pass laws in their favor.

As the American Economic Liberties Project reported, lobbying can work. Big corporations who lobby tend to have a higher return on equity and a higher market share than those who don't. On top of that, despite benefiting from our federal government, many major corporations aren't spreading the wealth by paying federal corporate income taxes that could go toward the public good.

In 2020, the nonprofit organization Public Citizen concluded that:

- The fifty-five largest corporations that paid no federal corporate income tax in 2020 collectively spent nearly $408 million on lobbying Congress.

- Given the federal corporate tax rate, they would have owed the federal government $8.5 billion without congressional tax breaks.

- Nearly all of these companies also benefited from tax giveaways from the feds, amounting to another $3.5 billion in tax rebates.

- So that's a total of $12 billion taxes avoided (or evaded) by these 55 companies!!

Okay, so major corporations are corporation-ing. Does this necessarily make our society undemocratic? What if the policies these companies lobby for don't really diverge from the interests of the average middle-class American? Some people argue that the general population gets the policies they want at least half of the time, so we're overstating the role of corporate influence on American democracy.

To be fair, while the sums of money being thrown around are large, their total impact on our federal policy is hard to measure, given that our capitalist American society was inherently structured around benefiting elites anyway, from the very beginning.

As I discussed in Chapter 4, the increasing influence of corporations on our politics and the decline of labor unions in the late 1960s and 70s substantially changed the life of workers in America for generations to come. As political scientist Lee Drutman observes, "rather than seeing government as a threat, [corporations] started looking to government as a potential source of profits and assistance." This is the essence of neoliberal capitalism.

So instead of thinking about lobbying as a precursor to corporate influence in politics, perhaps it's more helpful to think of lobbying as another outgrowth of already concentrated wealth and power—just one more institution that keeps churning the engine.

At best corporations are spending a ton of money that could go to much more useful things. Remember how that "Desperate Housewife" and Aunt Becky spent thousands of dollars to bribe their kids' way into the University of Southern California? Maybe it only slightly increased their kids' chances of admission, but the poors among us watching the drama from the sidelines pretty much agreed it was a huge waste of money and that rigging the system is patently unfair. Not to mention the fact that top schools already favor the wealthy and connected.

In the best-case scenario, where lobbying is only somewhat effective for the average corporation, it's pretty damn awful that really rich people (and corporations) have money like this to gamble with—always with the goal of making yet more money—while so much of the country is just trying to survive.

The theme here, as stated in Chapter 1, is that things may be relatively okay for a lot of us, but life could probably be much better with another system—a system where we prioritize the needs of people around us over what generates the most money for a few suits. We could have a system where the wealthy donor class and corporations aren't wastefully throwing cash around just for some measure of political influence—or even the illusion of influence, or their own ego trip. We could have an election process that doesn't capitalize on division, acrimony, and the unceasing culture wars prompted by elites' conservative allies in the capital.

Like, sure, you can fall for someone who accepted a bet just to date you. But what if you found someone who liked you as the nerdy, goofy person you've always been? We don't need capitalists who come up with manipulative schemes and hide the fine print (even if they eventually profess their love and leave us with a vintage car). We just want a real democracy.

cutting the strings

Well-known US socialists and organizations, like Bernie Sanders and the Democratic Socialists of America (DSA), have called for mandatory public financing to get big money out of politics. The DSA also urges the overturning of two Supreme Court cases: Citizens United v. Federal Election Commission (we parsed that legalese above) and Buckley v. Valeo, which also made it easier for big money donors to influence elections.

Through a public campaign-finance system, the government would match small donations. The ultimate goal is to engage everyday people in the election process and thus encourage them to help finance campaigns. For instance, starting in 2021, New York City's program allows any NYC resident to contribute $10 to a local campaign. The city program matches it eightfold, so that it's actually worth $90 to a candidate's campaign. As the NYC Campaign Finance Board puts it, this "empowers more candidates to run for office, even without access to wealth; ones who join can build viable, competitive campaigns for office by relying on support from their neighbors."

While NYC's matching program has spending limits in place, limits on campaign spending at the federal level are currently unconstitutional, thanks to the Supreme Court's recent decisions. Still, there are federal proposals for public campaign finance that promote a matching program, so that lesser-known candidates (*cough cough* scrappy socialists who can gin up grassroots donations maybe??) can have a shot.

And guess what: There is such an established program for presidential elections already, and most qualifying candidates participated in it from 1976–2004. The key step now is to actually fund it fully, after years of inadequate funding.

There have also been legislative proposals for the same kind of federal matching program for Congressional races that would offer 600 percent matching funds for smaller contributions and encourage more grassroots, less billionaire-backed campaigns. In the meantime, voters can also apply some pressure by supporting candidates that don't take corporate PAC money and refusing to back those that do.

In the same way a majority of capitalists narrow-mindedly focus on maximizing profit regardless of the horrible conditions their workers may face, far too many focus on profit to the detriment of our entire society. It doesn't matter if made-up culture wars engender more violence and division. It doesn't matter if children get slaughtered in mass shootings just by going to school. It doesn't matter if we fail to have a political system that reflects a lot of our policy preferences and if voices of the marginalized get muted. If these capitalists can maintain wealth and power, nothing else truly matters for them.

We keep hoping corporate politicians and their wealthy friends will give this country some dramatic makeover. And we keep voting for them, thinking that our lives will magically turn around and afford us a seat at the rich, cool kids' table. But way too many US politicians are stringing us along. There are, however, a few people—as you'll see in the next (and final!) chapter—who have been working to finally cut those ties. 🐷

10

Flip the Script

"IT'S NOT JUST THE COIN. IT'S 'THE KWAN.' IT
MEANS LOVE, RESPECT, COMMUNITY . . . AND THE
DOLLARS TOO. THE PACKAGE."
— ROD TIDWELL, *JERRY MAGUIRE*

Guy meets girl. Girl falls in love. Guy is a jerk. But by the end of this lopsided love story, she somehow convinces him that he, too, is madly in love, even though basically nothing about his character has changed.

We keep thinking we can win over the hotshot, womanizing (or manizing) capitalist. But in real life capitalists have whispered sweet nothings in our ears for over a century, playing a cat and mouse game that often ends in heartbreak. It's probably clear by now why we should move on from love interests who woo us with passionate speeches about how we complete them (a speech that just so happens to come only *after* we're ready to break up). But getting the strength to actually move on is another story. The best part of a breakup is your revenge era. You've been on a lil' fitness challenge. You have a better idea of what you want and don't want in a relationship. If you're really grown and mature, you've thought about the internal work necessary to do better the next go-round. Your whole aura is different. But it is work. So help me help you.

We met class warriors, revolutionary leaders, and activists who have all worked hard to create permanent solutions to the problems capitalism has created. Now we have to be our own fighters to get the glow up we all deserve.

Whether you're inclined to run for office, support co-ops and mutual aid programs where you live, or organize your coworkers, there are plenty of paths to take to chip away at capitalism's excesses and, eventually, hopefully transform the system altogether. We can all flip the tired, heartbreaking script. Thankfully, there are plenty of real-life sources of creative inspiration all around us.

fight the power

New York City Council Member Charles Barron was fielding calls from campaign staffers when we met on a warm day in East New York, a working-class Brooklyn neighborhood. After over twenty years of serving in state and local government, socialist and former Black Panther Barron's focus now was to lift up a new generation of Black radical politicians.

The Juneteenth holiday on which we spoke fell on Father's Day, and he's like the protective dad who grills his daughter's potential suitors before they get out the door on a first date. When millionaire developers and big box stores come knocking aggressively at the doors of politicians in an attempt to court them, Barron is an intimidating presence in the room—he makes them prove their worth. Often, they can't.

A real estate team that spent months trying to get city approval to build a massive mixed-use development in Harlem certainly couldn't get Barron's approval. As he excitedly recounted how the project was defeated, the drum he has been drumming for decades was loud and clear: socialists need state power.

Developers behind the One45 project wanted to erect a pair of towers in Harlem, one twenty-seven stories tall and another thirty-one stories, on 145th Street on the west side of the New York neighborhood. They included a new headquarters for Al Sharpton's nonprofit in the plans, a

"Power is the ability to make others respect the decisions you're making. And power is the ability for you to access resources for the betterment of your people. That's power."

— Charles Barron

carrot dangled to get community buy-in, and they got the support of the Council Speaker. Despite touting its affordability, developers of the project planned to price 80 percent of the housing units at the market rate. Even "affordable" housing subsidized by the government is not necessarily truly affordable for residents of the neighborhood. Local governments use a metric based on the area median income, or AMI. In New York City, that number is calculated by taking the median income of all five boroughs. So incomes of wealthier communities in the Upper East Side, for instance, are mixed in with low-income families in Harlem and the Bronx. The One45 project would have brought mostly market rate housing to a predominantly Black neighborhood where the income is below the city's median, while its average rent has soared to absurd levels.

"Go to your community board, I'm sure they'll be against it," Barron told the district's Council member Kristin Richardson Jordan. Then, he advised her, "tell the developers that you have an alternative plan. You'll do 17 stories, and 80 percent of the units have to be 30–50 percent of the AMI." This would keep the building at a roughly similar height to others nearby, and make it affordable to local residents, keeping further gentrification at bay.

In New York City, land use decisions typically defer to the Council member whose district would be impacted. Basically, Council members have the juice.

Jordan asked Barron to join a video call with developers when she presented the counterproposal. The developer immediately balked.

"Are you serious?" he scoffed at Jordan. "I don't even know how you can come up with something like that."

A large painting of Huey Newton flanks Council Member Barron as he recalls the meeting to me a few weeks later. He hasn't strayed far from the confrontational style the Panthers honed during the sixties. "Who the hell you think you talking to?" Barron had shot back. "You better not say a damn word for the rest of the meeting." The developer remained quiet as they continued.

Two weeks later, the developers backed out. The project was dead, and residents celebrated the fact that a megaproject that would only usher in expensive, market-rate housing for upper-income families could be successfully challenged.

"You beat Speaker Adams, Al Sharpton, and a multibillionaire developer," Barron told Jordan after the win. "You beat them! Power. That's power."

Power for progressives and socialists in just this one district means hundreds of families may have a better chance of affording a roof over their heads, in a city where capitalist greed has grossly inflated the rental market. Barron envisions using local electoral politics—and the resources of city government—for reforms that can ease the harms of capitalism. But his real goal is for everyday people to come together to replace our whole capitalist system with a socialist one, and he thinks state power and using municipal budgets can help us get there.

Government money is public money, and socialists can run for office to be stewards of that funding so that it truly serves the public instead of capitalists and their cronies. "We can't vote our way to freedom.

Flip the Script:
Charles Barron's Capitalism Breakup Guide

☐ Elect socialists to city and state legislatures, where land use and budget decisions are made.

☐ Invest public money in social programs and anti-capitalist projects, like community land trusts and worker cooperatives.

☐ Develop more democratic political bodies, such as people's assemblies, at a community level, so elected officials aren't making all the decisions.

☐ Show people their basic needs can be met with socialist reforms and the benefits of interacting with each other more communally through collective projects—like worker co-ops and CLTs. They will be then more inclined to support socialism and organize collectively against capitalism at a broader level.

The real power is in the masses. But their consciousness has to be raised up," he says. "We need millions engaged in collective action, other than just reacting to social issues that are plaguing our community." But he's aware that people won't be motivated by theoretical conversations.

"How do we implement concrete programs?" he asks rhetorically. "Power. None of this happens without power. Power is the ability to act. Power is the ability to make decisions in your best interest. Power is the ability to make others respect the decisions you're making. And power is the ability for you to access resources for the betterment of your people. That's power."

Fittingly, Barron cofounded a grassroots political organization called Operation P.O.W.E.R. ("People Organizing and Working for Empowerment and Respect") to create a pipeline for developing anti-capitalist Black elected officials and to build a base for socialist economic and political projects. Barron sees local budgets, like that of the City Council for New York City, as a tool for jumpstarting anti-capitalist programs. Community land trusts are just one example.

"Let's say that people support a community land trust out here in East New York. And we have one because of public funding," he notes.

With CLTs, people work together to decide how land is used, and they're required to keep housing affordable for residents who lease their home through a CLT. Like the Worker Self-Directed Enterprises Richard Wolff envisions that we discussed in Chapter 4, everyday people in CLTs—instead of a minority of people driven by profits or market share—make decisions, democratically. And if people who control our land—or jobs or healthcare or higher education—aren't primarily motivated by money, the community would likely benefit overall. "Once you start doing that from the bottom up and you show that it can work," Barron shares, "you can win people over ideologically. If you start on that kind of micro level, you can get people into the mindset that it's about collectivism and not individualism." Basically, you can start to untangle and discredit all the gaslighting and sweet talk we've heard in the past.

With the way the federal government moves (like, not at all) and how much the wealthy and big corporations have influence over it, seeing substantial progress through the presidency or Congress is a tall order. There was a glimmer of possibility recently, with the ascendence of Bernie Sanders and the popularity of Alexandria Ocasio-Cortez. But getting over the hump to sway hundreds of millions of people on a national level to commit to a socialist (and not get fearmongered out of it) could take some time, at least for presidential races.

A strategy to win state and local seats of power (like those on city councils, education boards, mayoralties, and state legislatures) for socialists could increase the likelihood that things actually get done. Preserving affordable housing, or using local money to fund community land trusts, Worker Self-Directed Enterprises, and cooperative banks, for instance, are just a few of those things.

flip the script: getting started

This whole book brought up big problems and big ideas. So where do we actually start? I've rounded up some US-based lefty organizations, people, and resources I've become familiar with in my own activist work. Whether you can support their offline organizing, learn from their online reading groups, or (unless Elon burns Twitter to the ground by the time you read this) read their really fire tweets for explanations of things, there's a place for you to get started. You don't have to leap into the socialism dating pool. You can dip a toe in. Put yourself out there!

Since this a post-pandemic book, of course you get a handy QR code with this list, and many more ways to get the socialist hookup, online:

horrible bosses

In the beginning of March 2020, something drew Christian Smalls to watch the news every day. "I was alarmed, but no one else was really serious about it," he tells me. "It" was a virus that would make New York City, where he had worked at Amazon's JFK8 warehouse, a deadly COVID-19 hotspot. His job didn't make him immune from the virus's spread.

"I started seeing everybody one by one become sick. One worker vomited at the station. Now you know the virus is definitely in the building. And they're trying to sugarcoat it by saying this is only one case," he says of company representatives. "I'm noticing several people just missing."

During a meeting later that month, he tells me, Amazon employees advised him not to tell anyone what he observed at the fulfillment center. That didn't sit right with him. "That was the last straw for me. I pretty much left that day and never came back as a supervisor."

For the rest of the week, Chris sat in the cafeteria, organizing his colleagues off the clock. That organizing led to a protest, where he called on the company to shut down the warehouse and allow workers to stay home, safe from the ravages of the mostly unknown disease.

He then expanded his activism beyond the warehouse, staging protests throughout New York City and bringing attention to the fundamental unfairness of seeing everyday workers face unsafe work conditions in a pandemic while Amazon rolled in record profits.

Chris's activism drew the attention of executives at the company. "He's not smart, or articulate," wrote Amazon's general counsel, David Zapolsky, in notes from a leadership meeting. "[A]nd to the extent the press wants to focus on us versus him, we will be in a much stronger PR position than simply explaining for the umpteenth time how we're trying to protect workers."

Chris wasn't an organizer by trade. His plan was to simply move up the ranks at work. He regularly commuted from Newark, New Jersey, to the Staten Island warehouse, carpooling with a coworker. During his first year working for the company, at a different warehouse, he didn't have a car, and it could take him up to three hours to travel.

Despite not having a college degree, he was a hard worker. He was promoted in 2015, within a year of starting at Amazon, advancing from a process assistant to a supervisory role. "It took me three years to realize Amazon's toxic culture. I was really praised my first year because I was really dedicated and pro-Amazon. They were selling me a dream the whole time."

Terminated from his job after Amazon said he was violating the company's COVID-19 safety protocols, Chris had time to commit full-time to organizing. He started an organization, the Congress of Essential Workers, to speak up for workers like him. "The capitalist economy of the US is built off the backs of a class of underpaid people who are degraded to wage laborers and valued only for what they produce, not for their intrinsic value as humans," its website reads. "We want to change this."

When Chris and I spoke in March 2021, a year after his first protest, it was clear he was thinking beyond the walls of JFK8. "We are the wealthy ones, if we really understood our power and our wealth. The workers are the ones who hold the value. Jeff Bezos don't come to the warehouse and pack these packages—it's us. If we stopped [working] for one day . . . and had a general strike, can you imagine the riptide that would go through this country? That will shake up every billionaire in this country—actually, all over the world."

While he drew the ire of top Amazon executives, Smalls attracted workers outside of the company who realized the potential to formally unionize one of the world's largest retailers. For years, Amazon notoriously had held outsized power, burning through workers without any need to make their work lives better. A union could change that, allowing workers to negotiate collectively for better wages, hours, and benefits.

It seemed like a pipe dream. Amazon had, from the beginning, successfully thwarted attempts to unionize with extremely aggressive tactics. But Smalls, and the growing collection of workers who joined him, would try anyway.

One of them was Cassio Mendoza. Cassio worked the night shift as a stower at JFK8. He's also a socialist. As Cassio began to organize with Christian to form Amazon's first union, he was careful not to rally his colleagues around his ideology. If people want to organize, he tells me, "first and foremost, be a really good worker who works hard to earn the respect of your coworkers." He adds: "[If] you seem like a lazy worker who doesn't really care about their job, other workers won't respect you, especially ones who ideologically don't agree with socialism, or communism or anything like that."

The scrappy crew of workers Chris led formally began the Amazon Labor Union, naming him president, sidestepping traditional union drive efforts and racking up wins along the way. They posted videos that went viral on TikTok. They helped coworkers who were in a financial pinch. "[G]o out of your way to do whatever you can to try to make people's lives easier—if you can help someone get their job back, or if you can help

Flip the Script:
Amazon Labor Union Organizer Cassio Mendoza on Organizing Your Coworkers

☐ If you're trying to unionize (especially at a huge company with large sums of money available to defeat your efforts), help your coworkers outside of the job. Fundraise for them or assist them in other ways that will help if they're going through something at home.

☐ There's no need to preach about being socialist. Instead, talk to them about specific financial struggles and needs. "You can't organize people through ideology," Cassio says. "You have to organize them based on the material needs that they have. So we would never talk about socialism. We would just talk about like, a living wage for all the workers or having our own organization deal with the fight for changes."

☐ Work hard and earn your coworkers' respect. If you're only there to unionize, other workers will be turned off.

All this stuff means actually getting offline, touching some grass, and talking IRL to the people you work with, fellow lefties!

them with something going on at home, or things like mutual aid, raising money for people. It depends on the situation, but just contribute whatever skills you have to make the movement stronger," Cassio shares.

Their tireless work paid off. On April 1, 2022, JFK8 became the first Amazon warehouse in the world to win an election to unionize. Additional steps would remain for them to officially become a union, including becoming legally certified by the National Labor Relations Board, an effort that Amazon expectedly challenged. But on that spring day in 2022—about two years after an employee with no organizing experience simply decided he was fed up—Chris, Cassio, and their colleagues could celebrate making history.

Chris wasn't armed with years of activism experience or Marxist theory. He just had grit and built connections. It helped make him a labor leader, but you don't even have to do all that. You can be a labor supporter. There have been hundreds of strikes over the past few years; working-class people are standing up to their capitalist bosses. Some of them have a strike fund, a pool of money workers tap into so they can protest their jobs (the only livelihood most people have) on the picket line and not be completely broke while doing so.

Even if you don't work in a traditional job that has a union or could organize, you can contribute to those funds for your friends' unions or the unions of companies whose goods you rely on. Show solidarity with other workers. The AFL-CIO has a whole list of them. Support a union if you do have one. If your job needs one because wages are crap and people are disenchanted, encourage your outspoken, hardworking friend to lead unionizing efforts.

Take inspo from one of the most influential organizers of the twentieth century, who cofounded a union with Cesar Chavez, and the Agricultural Workers Association, organizing strikes against capitalist landowners on behalf of farm workers. In 1966, Dolores Huerta was the first person in the US to negotiate a successful contract between farm workers and an agricultural company.

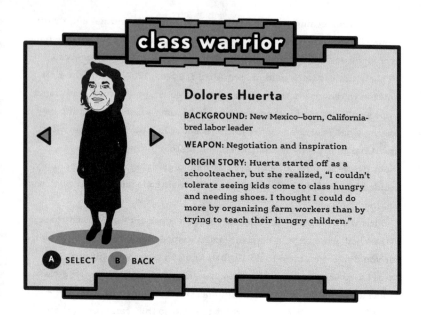

Dolores Huerta

BACKGROUND: New Mexico–born, California-bred labor leader

WEAPON: Negotiation and inspiration

ORIGIN STORY: Huerta started off as a schoolteacher, but she realized, "I couldn't tolerate seeing kids come to class hungry and needing shoes. I thought I could do more by organizing farm workers than by trying to teach their hungry children."

Ⓐ SELECT   Ⓑ BACK

choose your fighter

As much as capitalism is about power, it's also about everyday people. An elite group of überwealthy business owners and political leaders have come together to maintain systems that enrich them. Like Frederick Douglass said, "these bad boys aren't going to just ride their yachts into the sunset." Okay, he really said that "Power concedes nothing without a demand." But same same. Bourgeoisie millionaires and billionaires are comfortable and rich as hell; you think they'll give that up easily? So it's up to us to choose ourselves as our own class warriors and work with each other in the struggle.

The goal isn't a struggle for struggle's sake, but to make sure all of us can live comfortable lives. Sure, money is important. Despite what capitalists say (conveniently), we socialists want people to be financially comfortable, even your whack Uncle Larry. But there's also more to the world. Like, y'know, wanting that world to actually exist for the foreseeable future.

Socialists don't think that comfort should be exclusive to a minority and lorded over the rest of us, like some treasured reward in a twisted game that's impossible to win. Besides, what good is money if you're burnt out and unhappy, and a ton of other people you know are too? Like Cuba Gooding Jr.'s character Rod Tidwell told Jerry Maguire in . . . *Jerry Maguire*, "It's not just the coin. It's 'the kwan.' It means love, respect, community . . . and the dollars too." That's the balance Rod wanted in his life. And Jerry also wanted that kind of balance in his relationships with his clients (after all, that's what jumpstarts the whole movie).

I think about all the ups and downs my friends have gone through in dating (by "friends" I also mean me), but ultimately things ended up turning out how they wanted it. The relationships they have with their "forever person" may not be perfect. There are still challenges and quirks to work out and the occasional group-chat venting session. But I'm sure none of them want to go back to the wishy-washy, noncommittal, and downright toxic exes they had before. It's almost always scary moving on, but a lot of times it's worth it.

Socialism may not complete us and sweep us away in some whirlwind romance. But it may give us the comfort we haven't felt since capitalism forcefully weaseled its way into our lives. We owe it to ourselves, and future generations who are hoping for a habitable planet, to at least step out and give some other prospects a chance.

Acknowledgments

I thank all the people and institutions in my life that gave me a passion-ate sense of justice and paved my path to socialism in some way. First and foremost, my mother, who brought me into spaces with rich radical traditions. She handed me Assata Shakur's autobiography when I was ten for a fifth grade book report (yes, we were doing the most), encouraged me to do a sixth grade social science project on the Black Panther Party, brought me into the Malcolm X Grassroots Movement, introduced me to my godfather, former Panther Charles Barron, and opened my young mind to the Black Liberation Theology of the Pan African Orthodox Christian Church.

From this I had the bits and pieces to envision alternatives to our capitalist world, and in college I made a conscious choice to do something with it. That commitment, to work to improve the lives of the repressed, and Black communities in particular, probably would not have happened without the African American Studies department at my alma mater, Emory University. Thinking more critically about our history as a young adult made me more determined to see what small part I could play in the world to change our future.

I'm thankful to my Operation P.O.W.E.R. family, who helped me to continue to home in on and articulate my understanding of socialism and who gave me the space—and Black people the space—to dream of and fight for another way of life, free of capitalist exploitation.

This book was an absolute labor of love, and one that I would not have envisioned on my own. The idea of writing a book (my first book! with chapters! and illustrations!) was daunting. But I'm incredibly grateful to my editor, Madeline Jones, for reaching out to me with this opportunity and closely guiding me through this process. She's been encouraging, open to all of my many goofy ideas, and had the most patience in the world when I blew past many, many deadlines. But she remained supportive.

The illustrator and designer, Kayla E., has been an absolute rockstar. Her ability to convey the ideas I had in mind has really made this book come to life, and she cranked it out so beautifully on a tight timeline (given those missed deadlines of mine). Christopher Moisan, Algonquin Books' creative director, offered incredible design direction, helping to translate a ton of visual ideas into a cohesive final product that looks dope AF.

I'm grateful for my time in Milwaukee, where I wrote most of this book, and where I had some respite amid personal challenges. I had friends who kept me mentally balanced when life got rough. There were frequent FaceTimes, when the isolation of COVID-19 and being in a new city with no existing network tested my emotions (thank you Rayna!), and people who made me feel like I had family away from home (shout-out to Kristin).

Thank you to my agent, Tanya McKinnon, who had faith in me as an unproven author. Her commitment to diversifying the literary world is why you're reading this.

Thank you to the editors and mentors who helped me refine my writing and gave me the chance to publish without a traditional writing or journalism background: from Damon Young and Panama Jackson at Very Smart Brothas, to Christina Coleman and Cori Murray (formerly at Essence), to Amana Fontanella-Khan at the Guardian.

Lastly, I'd like to thank everyone who offered their time and insight for this book, as well as the ancestors who faced violence and alienation for their radical visions, laying the necessary foundation on which many of us socialists rest. For the living contributors to this book, I thank you: Charles Barron, Richard Wolff, Joshua Dedmond, Nina Turner, Astra Taylor, Raúl Carrillo, Thea Riofrancos, Cassio Mendoza and Christian Smalls. For those who are no longer with us—Claudia Jones, Lucy Parsons, Ella Baker, Kwame Nkrumah, Julius Nyerere, Patrice Lumumba, Maurice Bishop, W. E. B. Du Bois, Malcolm X, A. Philip Randolph, Bayard Rustin, Martin Luther King Jr., Lorraine Hansberry, Huey Newton, Bobby Seale, Fred Hampton, Kwame Ture, Chokwe Lumumba Sr., Eric Williams, Cedric Robinson, and many, many more—I, we, owe you so much. I hope generations to come continue the arduous work to which you dedicated your lives, until we finally get free.

Notes

CHAPTER 1.

Profit off many workers "Thus the whole historical movement is concentrated in the hands of the bourgeoisie" Marx, Karl, et al. *The Communist Manifesto* (first published Feb. 21, 1848, as *Das Kommunistische Manifest*), available at www.marxists.org/archive/marx/works/1848/communist-manifesto/ch01.htm#007.

Profit from labor "those who make their income chiefly by profit derived through the hiring of labor" Du Bois, W. E. B. *Black Reconstruction in America; an Essay Toward a History of the Part Which Black Folk Played in the Attempt to Reconstruct Democracy in America, 1860–1880*, New York: Antheum, 1969.

Resources Marx, Karl. *Economic Manuscripts: Capital Vol. I*, Chapter 7, https://www.marxists.org/archive/marx/works/1867-c1/ch07.htm.

"Commitment to making money" "The Two Nations of Black America," transcript of interview with Kathleen Cleaver, *Frontline*, Public Broadcasting Service, https://www.pbs.org/wgbh/pages/frontline/shows/race/interviews/kcleaver.html.

"No ethical relationship" Editorial team. "'The History of Indigenous People Is of Anti-Capitalist Resistance': An Interview with Nick Estes." *Regeneration Magazine*, no. 29 (June 2020), https://regenerationmag.org/our-history-is-the-future-interview-with-nick-estes/.

"Outlived its usefulness" King, Martin Luther, Jr. "Notes on American Capitalism." *The Martin Luther King, Jr., Research and Education Institute*, no. 21 (May 2021), https://kinginstitute.stanford.edu/king-papers/documents/notes-american-capitalism.

"10 percent of the wealthy" López, Carlos Andres. "Dolores Huerta: 'We Have to Keep on Marching.'" *New York Times*, Oct. 7, 2020, https://www.nytimes.com/2020/10/07/opinion/international-world/dolores-huerta-activists-unions.html.

Bargain for better "Right to Work," AFL-CIO, https://aflcio.org/issues/right-work.

Skewed distribution of wealth "the value of financial assets plus real assets (principally housing) owned by households, minus their debts." *Credit Suisse 2021 Global Wealth Report*, June 2021, accessed January 24, 2023, https://www.credit-suisse.com/about-us/en/reports-research/global-wealth-report.html.

Enslaved income inequality Williamson, Jeffrey G., and Peter Lindert. "Unequal Gains: American Growth and Inequality since 1700." Center for Economic Policy Research, June 16, 2016, https://voxeu.org/article/american-growth-and-inequality-1700.

The country's wealth the author's own calculations, based on Federal Reserve data: https://www.federalreserve.gov/releases/z1/dataviz/dfa/distribute/table/.

"What could be" Robinson, Nathan J. "Why Equality Is Indispensable." *Current Affairs*, no. 19 (Feb. 2018), https://www.currentaffairs.org/2018/02/why-equality-is-indispensable.

Replacement sources of wealth Rodney, Walter. *How Europe Underdeveloped Africa*, London: Bogle-L'Ouverhure Publications, 1978, p. 195.

Manufacturing city growth "with increased production came also a great increase in the population under the factory system, especially in certain districts. In 1700, Lancashire numbered only 166,200 inhabitants; in 1750 the population was 297,400; in 1801 it had grown to 672,565; in 1831 to 1,336,854." Price, George M. *The Modern Factory: Safety, Sanitation and Welfare*, New York: John Wiley & Sons, 1914.

Rise of capitalism Ibid.

Robinson, Cedric J. *Black Marxism: The Making of the Black Radical Tradition*, Chapel Hill: University of North Carolina Press, 2000.

Marx, Karl, et al. *The Communist Manifesto* (first published February 21, 1848 as *Das Kommunistische Manifest*), www.marxists.org/archive/marx/works/1848/communist -manifesto/ch01.htm#007.

More owner profits Ibid.

Wages fell Ibid.

Forced child labor Ibid.

Child suicide "those who make their income chiefly by profit derived through the hiring of labor" Du Bois, W. E. B. *Black Reconstruction in America; an Essay toward a History of the Part Which Black Folk Played in the Attempt to Reconstruct Democracy in America, 1860–1880*, New York: Antheum, 1969.

Marx, Karl, et al. *The Communist Manifesto* (first published February 21, 1848 as *Das Kommunistische Manifest*), www.marxists.org/archive/marx/works/1848/communist-manifesto/ch01.htm#007.

CHAPTER 2.

Toil on land Williams, Eric. *Capitalism and Slavery*, 3rd ed., Chapel Hill: University of North Carolina Press, 2021.

"World crisis" Du Bois, W. E. B. "Marxism and the Negro Problem." *The Crisis*, vol. 40, no. 5 (May 1933), pp. 103–104, 118.

"Competing with white workers" Harris, Leslie. *In the Shadow of Slavery: African Americans in New York City, 1626–1863*, Chicago: University of Chicago Press, 2004.

"Gaining power" Ibid.

Mob violence Ibid.

Riots forced hundreds Ibid.

A haunting picture "Newspaper Coverage of the 1863 New York City Draft Riots." NewseumED, the Freedom Forum, https://newseumed.org/tools/artifact/newspaper-coverage-1863-new-york-city-draft-riots.

Blow to capitalism Marx, Karl. "Address of the International Working Men's Association to Abraham Lincoln, President of the United States of America." *Marx & Engels Internet Archive*, 2000 (originally written 1865), https://www.marxists.org/archive/marx/iwma/documents/1864/lincoln-letter.htm.

"Infinitely worse" Du Bois, W. E. B. *Black Reconstruction in America: an Essay Toward a History of the Part Which Black Folk Played in the Attempt to Reconstruct Democracy in America, 1860–1880*, New York: Antheum, 1969.

"Own material interest" Ibid.

In the new deal Rothstein, Richard. *The Color of Law: A Forgotten History of How Our Government Segregated America*. New York: Liveright, 2018.

Losses for Black households Perry, Andre, et al. *2018 Annual Report—Brookings*, Metropolitan Policy Program at Brookings, Nov. 2018, https://www.brookings.edu/wp-content/uploads/2018/11/2018-annual-report.pdf.

No signs of stopping Derenoncourt, Ellora, Chi Hyun Kim, Moritz Kuhn, Moritz Schularick, "Wealth of Two Nations—The U.S. Racial Wealth Gap, 1860–2020," PrincetonEconomics, https://economics.princeton.edu/working-papers/wealth-of-two-nations-the-u-s-racial-wealth-gap-1860-2020/.

"Sixteenth century on" Robinson, Cedric J. *Black Marxism: The Making of the Black Radical Tradition*, Chapel Hill: University of North Carolina Press, 2000.

Ripped of contributions Ibid.

Rebellion across race lines "Jim Crow Laws." National Parks Service, U.S. Department of the Interior, https://www.nps.gov/malu/learn/education/jim_crow_laws.htm.

Western Europe's industrialization Du Bois, W. E. B. *Color and Democracy: Colonies and Peace*. Chesapeake, MD: ECA Associates, 1990.

Extract natural resources Nkrumah, Kwame, *Neo-colonialism: The Last Stage of Imperialism*, Nashville, TN: Thomas Nelson & Sons, 1965.

Profit from Asia and Africa Nkrumah, Kwame. *Revolutionary Path*, Bedford, UK: Panaf Books, 1973.

Limited to trading posts Rodney, Walter. *How Europe Underdeveloped Africa*, London: Verso Books, 2018.

"Scramble for Africa" Murray, Brian. "Building Congo, Writing Empire: The Literary Labours of Henry Morton Stanley." *English Studies in Africa*, vol. 59, no. 1 (2016), pp. 6–17, https://doi.org/10.1080/00138398.2016.1173271.

Colonized by Europeans "Story Map Journal." *Arcgis*, https://www.arcgis.com/apps/MapJournal/index.html?appid=6df9eef17b93493da8a1353777aa2a88#:~:text=Before.

Colonize 90 percent Ibid.

In their home countries Rodney, Walter. *How Europe Underdeveloped Africa*, London: Verso Books, 2018.

European counterparts Ibid.

Exploitation of colonies Ibid.

"Low wages of colored labor" Du Bois, W. E. B. "Socialism and the American Negro, April 9, 1960." *Credo*, Special Collections and University Archives, University of Massachusetts—Amherst Libraries, https://credo.library.umass.edu/view/full/mums312-b206-i053.

Global South labor Robinson, Cedric J. *Black Marxism: The Making of the Black Radical Tradition*, Chapel Hill: University of North Carolina Press, 2000, pp. 161.

Subordinate industrial interests Harris, Abram Lincoln. *The Negro as Capitalist: A Study* of *Banking and Business among American Negroes*, Whitefish, MT: Kessinger Publishing, 2010.

Richest people 2021 Dolan, Kerry A. "Forbes' 35th Annual World's Billionaires List: Facts and Figures 2021." *Forbes*, Apr. 6, 2021, https://www.forbes.com/sites/kerry-adolan/2021/04/06/forbes-35th-annual-worlds-billionaires-list-facts-and-figures-2021/?sh=254531975e58.

Already have access Darity Jr., William, Darrick Hamilton, Mark Paul, Alan Aja, Anne Price, Antonio Moore, and Caterina Chiopris. "What We Get Wrong About Closing the Racial Wealth Gap." *Narrow the Gap! Healing Communities, Reducing Disparities*, Samuel DuBois Cook Center on Social Equity, April 2018, https://socialequity.duke.edu/wp-content/uploads/2019/10/what-we-get-wrong.pdf.

Becoming self-employed Ibid.

Average self-employed family Headd, Brian. "Small Business Facts." *Small Business Administration Office of Advocacy*, Aug. 2021, https://cdn.advocacy.sba.gov/wp-content/uploads/2021/08/17095726/Small-Business-Facts-Business-Owner-Wealth.pdf.

"Economic Salvation" Harris, Abram Lincoln. *The Negro as Capitalist: A Study of Banking and Business among American Negroes*, Whitefish, MT: Kessinger Publishing, 2010.

CHAPTER 3.

Production in society Marx, Karl, et al. *The Communist Manifesto*, (first published Feb. 21, 1848, as *Das Kommunistische Manifest*), www.marxists.org/archive/marx/works/1848/communist-manifesto/ch01.htm#007.

How companies are run Wolff, Richard, *Democracy at Work: A Cure for Capitalism*, Chicago: Haymarket Books, 2012.

John R. Commons Commons, John R. *Myself: The Autobiography of J. R. Commons*, Madison: University of Wisconsin Press, 1964, p. 53.

"Wisconsin School" Kaufman, Bruce E. "John R. Commons and the Wisconsin School on Industrial Relations Strategy and Policy." *Industrial and Labor Relations Review* 57, no. 1 (2003), pp. 3–30. https://doi.org/10.2307/3590979.

Decision-making power Ibid.

First real social welfare Kaufman, Dan. *The Fall of Wisconsin: The Conservative Conquest of a Progressive Bastion and the Future of American Politics*, New York: W. W. Norton, 2018, p. 26.

Collective bargaining laws Brunner, Eric J., and Andrew Ju. "State Collective Bargaining Laws and Public-Sector Pay." *ILR Review*, vol. 72, no. 2 (2018), pp. 480–508, https://doi.org/10.1177/0019793918808727.

Radicalized through woodcarving Emil happened to be studying woodcarving in Germany not long after the German government passed anti-socialism laws (called the Exception Laws). He joined a woodcarving trade union, linked up with socialists who were striking and protesting the laws, started reading Marx, and boom, he came back to Wisconsin (where he was raised) full socialist. No wonder the right wing still goes balls to the wall trying to destroy unions. See *Socialist Campaign Book*, Chicago: National Headquarters Socialist Party, 1912, pp. 17–18.

Victor Berger "Representative Victor Berger of Wisconsin, the First Socialist Member of Congress." *US House of Representatives: History, Art & Archives*, https://history.house.gov/Historical-Highlights/1851-1900/Representative-Victor-Berger-of-Wisconsin,-the-first-Socialist-Member-of-Congress/.

Save capitalism Commons, John R. *Myself: The Autobiography of J.R. Commons*, Madison: University of Wisconsin Press, 1964, p. 143.

Replacement of capitalism "Milwaukee Sewer Socialism." Wisconsin Historical Society, Aug. 3, 2012, https://www.wisconsinhistory.org/Records/Article/CS428.

Daniel Hoan Booth, Douglas E. "Municipal Socialism and City Government Reform." *Journal of Urban History*, vol. 12, no. 1 (1985), pp. 51–74, https://doi.org/10.1177/009614 428501200103.

Doubling the park system Ibid.

Chokwe Lumumba, Sr. Umoja, Akinyele. "The People Must Decide: Chokwe Lumumba, New Black Power, and the Potential for Participatory Democracy in Mississippi." *The Black Scholar*, vol. 48, no. 2 (2018), pp. 7–19, https://doi.org/10.1080/000642 46.2018.1435126.

Economic tenets Umoja, Akinyele Omowale. *We Will Shoot Back: Armed Resistance in the Mississippi Freedom Movement*, New York: New York University Press, 2013, p. 190.

Participating in the strike Ceplair, Larry. "The Film Industry's Battle against Left-Wing Influences, from the Russian Revolution to the Blacklist." *Film History*, vol. 20, no. 4 (2008), pp. 399–411, accessed Feb. 12, 2023, JSTOR, http://www.jstor.org/stable/27670743.

White-collar jury Schneirov, Richard. "The Haymarket Bomb in Historical Context." *Northern Illinois University Digital Library*, 2016, https://digital.lib.niu.edu/illinois/gildedage/haymarket.

Raids of communist headquarters W. H. D. R. "The Status of Communists under Federal Law." *Virginia Law Review*, vol. 34, no. 4 (1948), pp. 439–450, accessed April 14, 2022, https://doi.org/10.2307/1068965.

Red scare press coverage Schmidt, Regin. *Red Scare: FBI and the Origins of Anticommunism in the United States, 1919–1943*, Copenhagen: Museum Tusculanum Press, 2000.

Spread right-wing propaganda Ibid.

Nothing new here Ibid.

"Pure, and blatant discrimination" National Highway Traffic Safety Administration. "Susie Healy–Comment." *Regulations*, Apr. 10, 1997, https://www.regulations.gov/comment/NHTSA-1997-2724-0663.

"If an SUV makes me happy" National Highway Traffic Safety Administration. "Multiple Submitters (25)—Comments." *Regulations*, Mar. 3, 2004, https://www.regulations.gov/comment/NHTSA-2003-16128-0247-0002.

"Very disappointing" Department of the Treasury. "Comment on FR Doc # 07-04914." *Regulations*, Oct. 15, 2007, https://www.regulations.gov/comment/TREAS-DO-2007-0015-0014.

To benefit capitalists Marx, Karl, et al. *The Communist Manifesto* (first published Feb. 21, 1848, as *Das Kommunistische Manifest*), www.marxists.org/archive/marx/works/1848/communist-manifesto/ch01.htm#007.

"Power to subjugate" Ibid.

"Bourgeoisie private property" Ibid.

"Destroying it daily" Ibid.

"Became more popular" Salmon, Felix. "America's Continued Move Toward Socialism." *Axios*, June, 25, 2021, https://www.axios.com/americas-continued-move-toward-socialism-84a0dda7-4b8d-483a-8c4e-0c2e562c4e67.html.

CHAPTER 4.

Trends in the Minimum Wage Baker, Dean. "Correction: This Is What Minimum Wage Would Be If It Kept Pace with Productivity." *Center for Economic and Policy Research*, Mar. 16, 2022, https://cepr.net/this-is-what-minimum-wage-would-be-if-it-kept-pace-with-productivity/.

Take Me Back to 1973 "The Productivity–Pay Gap." *Economic Policy Institute*, Oct. 2022, https://www.epi.org/productivity-pay-gap/.

Keeping up with cost Stansbury, Anna, and Lawrence H. Summers. "The Declining Worker Power Hypothesis: An Explanation for the Recent Evolution of the American Economy." *Brookings Papers on Economic Activity*, Washington, DC: Brookings Institution Press, 2020, https://www.brookings.edu/wp-content/uploads/2020/12/StansburySummers-Final-web.pdf.

Keeping up with productivity "The Productivity–Pay Gap." *Economic Policy Institute*, Oct. 2022, https://www.epi.org/productivity-pay-gap/. Economic Policy Institute notes that: "Starting in the late 1970s, policymakers began dismantling all the policy bulwarks helping to ensure that typical workers' wages grew with productivity. Excess unemployment was tolerated to keep any chance of inflation in check. Raises in the federal minimum wage became smaller and rarer. Labor law failed to keep pace with growing employer hostility toward unions. Tax rates on top incomes were lowered. And anti-worker deregulatory pushes—from the deregulation of the trucking and airline industries to the retreat of anti-trust policy to the dismantling of financial regulations and more—succeeded again and again."

1974 median annual income Richardson, Elliot L., and Robert L. Hogan. "Statistical Abstract of the United States, Prepared by the Chief of the Bureau of Statistics, Treasury Department. 1976." Ann Arbor, MI: HathiTrust, 1974, https://babel.hathitrust.org/cgi/pt?id=mdp.39015021301612&view=1up&seq=406.

$66,415 today "CPI Inflation Calculator." U.S. Bureau of Labor Statistics, http://www.bls.gov/data/inflation_calculator.htm.

2020 median annual income "Measures of Central Tendency for Wage Data." Average Wages, Median Wages, and Wage Dispersion, Social Security Administration, https://www.ssa.gov/oact/cola/central.html.

Execute-labor-organizers e.g., the Haymarket Affair executions.

In a union Dickens, William, and Jonathan Leonard. "Accounting for the Decline in Union Membership." *National Bureau of Economic Research Working Paper Series*, vol. 38, no. 2 (1984), pp. 323–34, https://doi.org/10.3386/w1275.

Build unity and organize "The Productivity–Pay Gap." *Economic Policy Institute*, Oct. 2022, https://www.epi.org/productivity-pay-gap/.

Intimidation tactics Domhoff, G. William. "Power in America." *Who Rules America: The Rise and Fall of Labor Unions in the U.S.*, G. William Domhoff, 2022, https://whorulesamerica.ucsc.edu/power/history_of_labor_unions.html.

Disproportionate Black employment   "Milwaukee Sewer Socialism." Wisconsin Historical Society, no. 3 (Aug. 2012), https://www.wisconsinhistory.org/Records/Article/CS428.

Ongoing employment discrimination   "March on Washington for Jobs and Freedom; Part 8 of 17", WGBH Open Vault archive, GBH, 2020, https://openvault.wgbh.org/catalog/A_27BB06E300874F279030125D1216C8B5.

Domhoff continues   Domhoff, G. William. "Power in America." Who Rules America: The Rise and Fall of Labor Unions in the U.S., G. William Domhoff, 2022, https://whorulesamerica.ucsc.edu/power/history_of_labor_unions.html.

Jobs risk being offshored   Devaraj, Srikant, et al. "How Vulnerable Are American Communities to Automation, Trade, & Urbanization?" Ball State University CBER & Rural Policy Research Institute, June 19, 2017, https://projects.cberdata.org/reports/Vulnerability-20170719.pdf.

China's hourly minimum wage   Norden, William, and Emmanuel Elone. "China Provinces Increase Minimum Wages." Bloomberg Tax, Bloomberg Industry Group, Sept. 10, 2021, https://news.bloombergtax.com/payroll/chinese-provinces-increase-minimum-wages.

Mexico's and India's minimum wage   Boesler, Matthew. "Here's How America's Minimum Wage Stacks up against Countries like India, Russia, Greece, and France." Business Insider, Aug. 19, 2013, https://www.businessinsider.com/a-look-at-minimum-wages-around-the-world-2013-8.

"Temporary" full employment   Ibid.

Billionaires' $5 trillion   Vega, Nicholas. "Billionaires Made $5 Trillion in the Past Year—and Their Wealth Is Growing at an 'Unprecedented' Rate." CNBC, Jan. 19, 2022, https://www.cnbc.com/2022/01/19/worlds-billionaires-made-5-trillion-dollars-over-the-past-year.html.

Ten richest men   Gleeson, Scott. "World's 10 Richest Men Double Wealth in the Pandemic While 99% of Incomes Drop, Group Says." USA Today, Gannett Satellite Information Network, Jan. 18, 2022, https://www.usatoday.com/story/money/2022/01/18/richest-men-world-doubled-income-covid-pandemic/6561147001/.

Surpasses the Gilded Age   Vega, Nicholas. "Billionaires Made $5 Trillion in the Past Year-and Their Wealth Is Growing at an 'Unprecedented' Rate." CNBC, Jan. 19, 2022, https://www.cnbc.com/2022/01/19/worlds-billionaires-made-5-trillion-dollars-over-the-past-year.html.

Increase in wage inequality   "The Impact of Manufacturing Employment Decline on Black and White Americans." Centre For Economic Policy Research, Dec. 19, 2018, https://cepr.org/voxeu/columns/impact-manufacturing-employment-decline-black-and-white-americans.

Intelligent, militant group   Randolph, A. Philip. "Our Reason for Being." Messenger, August 1919, 11–12, available at http://historymatters.gmu.edu/d/5125.

Vulnerable workers of color   Stringer, Scott M. "New York City's Frontline Workers." Office of the New York City Comptroller, Mar. 2020, https://comptroller.nyc.gov/reports/new-york-citys-frontline-workers/.

Great Resignation   "Table 4. Quits Levels and Rates by Industry and Region, Seasonally Adjusted— 2022 M12 Results." U.S. Bureau of Labor Statistics, 1 Feb. 2023, https://www.bls.gov/news.release/jolts.t04.htm.

Labor protests and strikes   "Labor Action Tracker." *ILR Labor Action Tracker*, Cornell Industrial and Labor Relations School, https://striketracker.ilr.cornell.edu/.

California fast food workers   AFL-CIO Staff. "A.B. 257 Is a Big Step Forward for California Fast-Food Workers: AFL-CIO." AFL-CIO, American Federation of Labor Congress of Industrial Organization, Sept. 7, 2022, https://aflcio.org/2022/9/7/ab-257-big-step-forward-california-fast-food-workers.

Approval of labor unions   McCarthy, Justin. "U.S. Approval of Labor Unions at Highest Point since 1965." *Gallup*, Jan. 25, 2023, https://news.gallup.com/poll/398303/approval-labor-unions-highest-point-1965.aspx.

CHAPTER 5.

Black Panther Party   Hilliard, David, and Dr. Huey P. Newton Foundation. *The Black Panther Party: Service to the People Programs*, Albuquerque: University of New Mexico Press, 2008.

Multimillion-dollar campaigns   Cancryn, Adam. "The Army Built to Fight 'Medicare for All.'" POLITICO, 25 Nov. 2019, https://www.politico.com/news/agenda/2019/11/25/medicare-for-all-lobbying-072110.

Replacing private health insurance   Clement, Scott, et al. "Exit Polls from the 2020 South Carolina Democratic Primary." *Washington Post*, Mar. 1, 2020, https://www.washingtonpost.com/graphics/politics/exit-polls-2020-south-carolina-primary/.

Without suffering hardship   "Universal Health Coverage." World Health Organization, April 7, 2019, https://www.who.int/publications/i/item/universal-health-coverage.

Single payer healthcare   Christopher, Andrea S. "Single Payer Healthcare: Pluses, Minuses, and What It Means for You." *Harvard Health*, June 27, 2016, https://www.health.harvard.edu/blog/single-payer-healthcare-pluses-minuses-means-201606279835.

Under one plan   Ibid.

Coordinated healthcare system   Kliff, Sarah. "Covid Medical Bills Are about to Get Bigger." *New York Times*, Sept. 2, 2021, https://www.nytimes.com/2021/09/02/upshot/covid-medical-bills.html.

Fears of desegregation   "Timeline: History of Health Reform in the U.S." Kaiser Family Foundation, 2011, https://kff.org/wp-content/uploads/2011/03/5-02-13-history-of-health-reform.pdf.

Proposals for nationalized insurance   Thomas, Karen Kruse. *The Wound of My People: Segregation and the Modernization of Healthcare in North Carolina, 1935–1975*, Ann Arbor: ProQuest Dissertations Publishing, 1999.

Progressive Party platform   Murray, John E. *Origins of American Health Insurance: A History of Industrial Sickness Funds*, New Haven, CT: Yale University Press, 2008, p. 16.

Share the costs   Palmer, Karen S. "A Brief History: Universal Health Care Efforts in the US." PNHP, Physicians for a National Health Program, May 3, 2021, https://pnhp.org/a-brief-history-universal-health-care-efforts-in-the-us/.

Commercial life insurance opposition   Ibid.

"Anti-American" insurance   Ibid; "Anti-German Sentiment." *Digital History*, 2021, https://www.digitalhistory.uh.edu/disp_textbook.cfm?smtid=2&psid=3478; Fischer,

Nick. "The Committee on Public Information and the Birth of US State Propaganda." *Australasian Journal of American Studies*, vol. 35, no. 1 (2016) pp. 51–78, JSTOR, accessed Feb. 13, 2023, http://www.jstor.org/stable/44779771.

Usher in socialism Boychuk, Gerard William. *National Health Insurance in the United States and Canada: Race, Territory, and the Roots of Difference*, Washington, DC: Georgetown University Press, 2008, pp. 42–52.

Requiring Americans get covered Institute of Medicine. "Appendix F: Key Features of the Affordable Care Act by Year." *The Impacts of the Affordable Care Act on Preparedness Resources and Programs: Workshop Summary*, Washington, DC: National Academies Press, 2014, available at: https://www.ncbi.nlm.nih.gov/books/NBK241401/.

Very chill reactions Bizzle, Martha, et al. "The Specter of Socialized Medicine." Center for American Progress, May 14, 2008, https://www.americanprogress.org/article/the-specter-of-socialized-medicine/.

"Social Security 'Communist Plot,' Medicare Called Government Takeover." Communications Workers of America, 1 Sept. 1, 2009, https://cwa-union.org/news/entry/social_security_communist_plot_medicare_called_government_takeover.

Russian gulag Moser, Whet. "How the AMA Scared Us Away from 'Socialized Medicine' and Prepared Us for Obamacare." *Chicago Magazine*, Chicago Tribune Media Group, Oct. 19, 2012, https://www.chicagomag.com/city-life/october-2012/how-the-ama-scared-us-away-from-socialized-medicine-and-prepared-us-for-obamacare/.

Truman's national health plan "Congressional Record." Congress.gov, Library of Congress, https://www.congress.gov/congressional-record/82nd-congress/browse-by-date.

Ronald Reagan "Ronald Reagan Speaks out on Socialized Medicine—Audio." Ronald Reagan Foundation, available at YouTube.com, July 23, 2009, accessed Feb. 13, 2023, https://www.youtube.com/watch?v=AYrlDlrLDSQ.

George H. W. Bush U.S. Government Publishing Office. "Remarks to the Staff of the University Medical Center of Southern Nevada in Las Vegas, Nevada." *Public Papers of the Presidents of the United States: George H. W. Bush (1992, Book I)*, Feb. 6, 1992, https://www.govinfo.gov/content/pkg/PPP-1992-book1/html/PPP-1992-book1-doc-pg209.htm.

USSR was not socialist Fitzgibbons, Daniel J. "USSR Strayed from Communism, Say Economics Professors." *The Campus Chronicle*, University of Massachusetts–Amherst, Oct. 11, 2002, https://www.umass.edu/pubaffs/chronicle/archives/02/10-11/economics.html.

Linera, Álvaro García. "Former Bolivian VP Álvaro García Linera on How Socialists Can Win." Translated by Nicholas Allen, Jacobin, May 4, 2021, https://jacobin.com/2021/04/interview-alvaro-garcia-linera-mas-bolivia-coup.

Rising medical costs Chapin, Christy Ford. *Ensuring America's Health: The Public Creation of the Corporate Health Care System*, Cambridge: Cambridge University Press, 2017.

Our life expectancy "Health Status—Life Expectancy at Birth—OECD Data." The OECD, https://data.oecd.org/healthstat/life-expectancy-at-birth.htm.

Pauper "race" Grau, María. "High-quality Universal Public Healthcare: Beneficial for Patients and Much More." *European Journal of Preventive Cardiology*, vol 29, no. 6 (April 2022), pp 913–15, available at https://doi.org/10.1093/eurjpc/zwab107.

Concentrated poverty Goetz, Edward G., et al. "Racially Concentrated Areas of Affluence: A Preliminary Investigation." *Cityscape*, vol. 21, no. 1 (2019), pp. 99–124, JSTOR, accessed Feb. 13, 2023, https://www.jstor.org/stable/26608013.

Harmful toxins Wodtke, Geoffrey T., et al. "Toxic Neighborhoods: The Effects of Concentrated Poverty and Environmental Lead Contamination on Early Childhood Development." *Demography*, vol. 59, no. 4 (2022), pp. 1275–98, https://doi.org/10.1215/00703370-10047481.

Kravitz-Wirtz, Nicole, et al. "Early-Life Air Pollution Exposure, Neighborhood Poverty, and Childhood Asthma in the United States, 1990–2014." *International Journal of Environmental Research and Public Health*, vol. 15, no. 6 (2018), p. 1114, https://doi.org/10.3390/ijerph15061114.

"Peculiar to negroes" Caplan, Arthur L., and Samuel Cartwright. "Report on the Diseases and Physical Peculiarities of the Negro Race." *Health, Disease, and Illness: Concepts in Medicine*, Washington, DC: Georgetown Univ. Press, 2004.

"Dysaesthesia aethiopica" Bailey, Zinzi D., et al. "How Structural Racism Works—Racist Policies as a Root Cause of U.S. Racial Health Inequities." *New England Journal of Medicine*, vol. 384, no. 8 (2021), pp. 768–73, https://doi.org/10.1056/nejmms2025396.

Haywood argued that Thomas, Karen Kruse. *Deluxe Jim Crow: Civil Rights and American Health Policy, 1935–1954*, Athens: University of Georgia Press, 2011.

As a constitutional right Article 43 of the Spanish Constitution of 1978: "Boe-A-2023-6374." Scribd, Agencia Estatal Boletín Oficial Del Estado, 27 Dec. 1978, p. 17, https://www.boe.es/legislacion/documentos/ConstitucionINGLES.pdf.

99.1 percent covered Bernal-Delgado, Enrique, et al. "Spain: Health System Review." *Health Systems in Transition*, vol. 20, no. 2 (2018), https://www.euro.who.int/__data/assets/pdf_file/0008/378620/hit-spain-eng.pdf.

Purchase additional insurance Bueno, Héctor, and Beatriz Pérez-Gómez. "Cardiovascular Health, Disease, and Care in Spain." *Circulation*, vol. 140, no. 1 (2019), pp. 13–15, https://doi.org/10.1161/circulationaha.119.038714.

Covered services are free "Spain Moves towards a More Resilient Health Coverage Policy during COVID-19." World Health Organization, Feb. 24, 2021, https://www.who.int/europe/news/item/24-02-2021-spain-moves-towards-a-more-resilient-health-coverage-policy-during-covid-19.

Out of pocket Dalmau-Bueno, Albert, et al. "Frequency of Health-Care Service Use and Severity of Illness in Undocumented Migrants in Catalonia, Spain: A Population-Based, Cross-Sectional Study." *The Lancet Planetary Health*, vol. 5, no. 5 (2021), https://doi.org/10.1016/s2542-5196(21)00036-x.

Highly regulated industry Bernal-Delgado, Enrique, et al. "Spain: Health System Review." *Health Systems in Transition*, vol. 20, no. 2 (2018), https://www.euro.who.int/__data/assets/pdf_file/0008/378620/hit-spain-eng.pdf.

Choose primary care physician Kringos, Dionne S., et al. *Building Primary Care in a Changing Europe: Case Studies*, Copenhagen: European Observatory on Health Systems and Policies, 2015.

Spain's life expectancy "Health Status—Life Expectancy at Birth." Organization for Economic Co-operation and Development, https://data.oecd.org/healthstat/life-expectancy-at-birth.htm.

CHAPTER 6.

Homeownership affordability Engels, Friedrich. The Housing Question, New York: International Publishers, 2021, p. 48.

Limited equity housing cooperatives "Limited Equity Cooperatives." Local Housing Solutions, NYU Furman Center, Sept. 24, 2022, https://localhousingsolutions.org/housing-policy-library/limited-equity-cooperatives/; Ortiz, Lillian M. "Will Limited-Equity Cooperatives Make a Comeback?" Shelterforce, Apr. 25, 2017, https://shelterforce.org/2017/04/25/will-limited-equity-co-ops-make-comeback/.

Singapore public housing "Public Housing—a Singapore Icon." Housing and Development Board, Government of Singapore, https://www.hdb.gov.sg/about-us/our-role/public-housing-a-singapore-icon.

Developed by the government Ibid.

Prevent investors from flipping "Do HDB Flat Buyers Own Their Flat?" Government of Singapore, 26 Aug. 2017, https://www.gov.sg/article/do-hdb-flat-buyers-own-their-flat.; Goh, Kian. Singapore Public Housing—Envisioning a State of Resilience, case study, Resilient Cities Housing Initiative at MIT, Mar. 5, 2014, https://static1.squarespace.com/static/5787b70d29687fd4e14dff41/t/595032f1b6ac-5081d705a247/1498428150395/SingaporeCaseStudy.pdf.

Maintain affordability Ibid.

Outlive the lease term "A Home for Everyone: Singapore's Public Housing." Government of Singapore, June 12, 2020, https://www.gov.sg/article/a-home-for-everyone-singapores-public-housing.

Getting Paid Enough "Housing Cost Burden for Low-Income Renters Has Increased Significantly in Last Two Decades." National Low Income Housing Coalition, July 6, 2020, https://nlihc.org/resource/housing-cost-burden-low-income-renters-has-increased-significantly-last-two-decades.

Super-luxury home sales Tarmy, James. "Super-Luxury Home Sales Surge across America, Rising 35% in 2021." Bloomberg.com, Dec. 21, 2021, https://www.bloomberg.com/news/articles/2021-12-21/super-luxury-home-sales-surged-across-america-rising-35-in-2021.

New class of property Ibid.

Increased homelessness The 2022 Annual Homelessness Assessment Report (AHAR) to Congress, The U.S. Department of Housing and Urban Development, Dec. 2022, https://www.huduser.gov/portal/sites/default/files/pdf/2022-AHAR-Part-1.pdf.

US eviction filings "HC3.3. Evictions," OECD Affordable Housing Database, Organisation for Economic Co-operation and Development, May 27, 2021, https://www.oecd.org/els/family/HC3-3-Evictions.pdf.

CoreLogic Malone, Thomas. "Single-Family Investor Activity Stalls in the Fourth Quarter of 2021." CoreLogic, May 16, 2022, https://www.corelogic.com/intelligence/find-stories/single-family-investor-activity-stalls-in-the-fourth-quarter-of-2021/.

Focused on low-priced homes Kasakove, Sophie. "Why the Road Is Getting Even Rockier for First-Time Home Buyers." New York Times, Apr. 23, 2022, https://www.nytimes.com/2022/04/23/us/corporate-real-estate-investors-housing-market.html.

Investor-purchased homes Schaul, Kevin, and Jonathan O'Connell. "Investors

Bought a Record Share of Homes in 2021. See Where." *Washington Post*, Feb. 16, 2022, https://www.washingtonpost.com/business/interactive/2022/housing-market-investors/.

Who are America's homeowners?   DeSilver, Drew. "As National Eviction Ban Expires, a Look at Who Rents and Who Owns in the U.S." Pew Research Center, Aug. 3, 2021, https://www.pewresearch.org/fact-tank/2021/08/02/as-national-eviction-ban-expires-a-look-at-who-rents-and-who-owns-in-the-u-s/; "U.S. Census Bureau Quickfacts: United States." US Census Bureau, United States Government, https://www.census.gov/quickfacts/fact/table/US/PST045221.

Racial homeownership gap   Warnock, Rob. "Apartment List's 2021 Millennial Homeownership Report." ApartmentList.com, Feb. 9, 2021, https://www.apartmentlist.com/research/millennial-homeownership-2021.

Racial disparities   Rothstein, Richard. *The Color of Law: A Forgotten History of How Our Government Segregated America*, New York: Liveright, 2018.

Weeks on Chart   "Techwood Homes," Historic American Buildings Survey, National Park Service-Southeast Region, Sept. 22, 1995, https://memory.loc.gov/master/pnp/habshaer/ga/ga0600/ga0662/data/ga0662data.pdf. Techwood Homes was the first federal public housing project. Constructed in Atlanta in 1935, it was originally whites-only.

Weingroff, Richard. "Federal-Aid Highway Act of 1956: Creating The Interstate System," US Department of Transportation, 1996, https://highways.dot.gov/public-roads/summer-1996/federal-aid-highway-act-1956-creating-interstate-system.

Homeownership ostensibly creates wealth   Darity Jr., William, Darrick Hamilton, Mark Paul, Alan Aja, Anne Price, Antonio Moore, and Caterina Chiopris. "What We Get Wrong About Closing the Racial Wealth Gap." *Narrow the Gap! Healing Communities, Reducing Disparities*, Samuel DuBois Cook Center on Social Equity, Apr. 2018, https://narrowthegap.org/images/documents/Wealth-Gap---FINAL-COMPLETE-REPORT.pdf

Taxed more for luxury   Stribling-Kivlan, Elizabeth Ann. "Against a Pied-a-Terre Tax." *New York Daily News*, Mar. 21, 2019, https://www.nydailynews.com/opinion/ny-oped-against-a-pied-a-terre-tax-20190322-2xkjl2572fghzpnuevu4g7lbmi-story.html.

Not an acute minority   "Homeownership Rate in the United States." FRED, Federal Reserve Bank of St. Louis, Jan. 31, 2023, https://fred.stlouisfed.org/series/RHORUSQ156N.

CHAPTER 7.

Most household debt ever   "U.S. Household Debt Tops $16 Trillion amid Rising Inflation." *Reuters*, Thomson Reuters, Aug. 2, 2022, https://www.reuters.com/markets/us/us-household-debt-tops-16-trillion-amid-rising-inflation-2022-08-02/.

Highest personal debts   "Quarterly Report on Household Debt and Credit." Center for Microeconomic Data, Federal Reserve Bank of New York, May 2022, https://www.newyorkfed.org/medialibrary/interactives/householdcredit/data/pdf/HHDC_2022Q1.

Student loan debt   "Distribution of Household Wealth in the U.S. since 1989." Board of Governors of the Federal Reserve System, federalreserve.gov, Dec. 16, 2022, https://www.federalreserve.gov/releases/z1/dataviz/dfa/distribute/table/.

Outstanding student loan debt Swagel, Philip L. "The Volume and Repayment of Federal Student Loans: 1995 to 2017." Congressional Budget Office, Nov. 2020, https://www.cbo.gov/publication/56754.

Rising college education costs "Deeper in Debt: Women & Student Loans." American Association of University Women, 26 Aug. 2021, https://www.aauw.org/resources/research/deeper-in-debt/.

Race and gender debt disparities Ibid.

Black students borrow more Ibid.

Largest student loan company "Customer Disservice: Examining Maximus, the Federal Contractor That Became the Largest Student Loan Company in the World." Student Borrower Protection Center, Mar. 2022, https://protectborrowers.org/wp-content/uploads/2022/03/CWA_SBPC_MAXIMUS.pdf.

Borrow from the feds "Who's My Student Loan Servicer?" Federal Student Aid, U.S. Department of Education, https://studentaid.gov/manage-loans/repayment/servicers.

Additional $500 billion Williams, Lance, and James B. Steele. "Who Got Rich off the Student Debt Crisis?" *Reveal*, June 28, 2016, https://revealnews.org/article/who-got-rich-off-the-student-debt-crisis/.

Underlying asset-generating money Bailey, Samantha L., and Christopher J. Ryan. "The Next 'Big Short': COVID-19, Student Loan Discharge in Bankruptcy, and the SLABS Market." Dedman School of Law, Southern Methodist University, Jan. 2020, https://scholar.smu.edu/cgi/viewcontent.cgi?article=4867&context=smulr.

SoFi Super Bowl stadium Fischer, Ben. "Naming-rights deal for L.A. stadium gives SoFi 'unprecedented' assets." *Sports Business Journal*, Sept. 9, 2019. SoFi paid over $600 million for the naming rights to the NFL's Inglewood stadium, if you were wondering. I heard* that each blade of astroturf bears the name of a student-loan borrower written in tiny font. What an honor! (*I made that up.)

Even if they go bankrupt 11 U.S.C. § 523(a)(8), US Bankruptcy Code, available at https://usbankruptcycode.org/chapter-5-creditors-the-debtor-and-the-estate/sub-chapter-ii-debtors-duties-and-benefits/section-523-exceptions-to-discharge/.

Payday loans Charron-Chénier, Raphaël. "Predatory Inclusion in Consumer Credit: Explaining Black and White Disparities in Payday Loan Use." *Sociological Forum*, vol. 35, no. 2 (May 2020), pp. 370–392, https://doi.org/10.1111/socf.12586.

Payday lender fees Hoevelmann, Kaitlyn. "How Payday Loans Work." *Saint Louis Fed Eagle*, Federal Reserve Bank of St. Louis, Dec. 28, 2021, https://www.stlouisfed.org/open-vault/2019/july/how-payday-loans-work.

APR for credit cards "Consumer Credit—G.19." Board of Governors of the Federal Reserve System, federalreserve.gov, Feb. 7, 2023, https://www.federalreserve.gov/releases/g19/current/.

Predatory inclusion Taylor, Keeanga-Yamahtta. "Race for Profit: How Banks and the Real Estate Industry Undermined Black Homeownership." *Journal of Urban Affairs*, vol. 43, no. 6 (Jan. 27, 2021), pp. 922–924, https://doi.org/10.1080/07352166.2020.1868257.

Charron-Chénier, Raphaël. "Predatory Inclusion in Consumer Credit: Explaining Black and White Disparities in Payday Loan Use." *Sociological Forum*, vol. 35, no. 2 (May 2020), pp. 370–392, https://doi.org/10.1111/socf.12586.

Builds on racial exclusion Baradaran, Mehrsa. "It's Time for Postal Banking." *Harvard Law Review*, no. 24 (Feb. 2014), https://harvardlawreview.org/2014/02/its-time-for-postal-banking/#_ftnref2.

Financialization Fischer, Amanda. "The Rising Financialization of the U.S. Economy Harms Workers and Their Families, Threatening a Strong Recovery." *Equitable Growth*, May 11, 2021, https://equitablegrowth.org/the-rising-financialization-of-the-u-s-economy-harms-workers-and-their-families-threatening-a-strong-recovery/.

Carceral debt Galindo, Manuel, and Hannah Appel. "Let's Get Free: Bail Debt, Pretrial Freedom, and Debtors' Unions." *South Atlantic Quarterly*, vol. 121, no. 4 (Oct. 1, 2022), pp. 865–71, https://doi.org/10.1215/00382876-10066580.

Jabali, Malaika. "Nonprofit Announces New App That Could Abolish $500 Million of Bail Debt for California Residents." *Essence*, Oct. 29, 2021, https://www.essence.com/news/nonprofit-announces-new-app-that-could-abolish-500-million-of-bail-debt-for-california-residents.

Created or worsened by legal system Ibid.

Median bail amount Lockwood, Beatrix, and Annaliese Griffin. "The System: The Ins and Outs of Bail." The Marshall Project, Oct. 28, 2020, https://www.themarshallproject.org/2020/10/28/the-ins-and-outs-of-bail.

Nonrefundable bail bond fee Onyekwere, Adureh. "How Cash Bail Works." Brennan Center for Justice, Feb. 24, 2021, https://www.brennancenter.org/our-work/research-reports/how-cash-bail-works#:~:text=If%20a%20defendant%20is%20unable,percent%20of%20the%20bail%20amount.

Court appearance contracts Ibid.

Released before trial Ibid.

Commercial bail system Preston, Allie. "Fact Sheet: Profit over People: Inside the Commercial Bail Bond Industry Fueling America's Cash Bail Systems." Center for American Progress, July 13, 2022, https://www.americanprogress.org/article/fact-sheet-profit-over-people/.

Monetary bail system burden Lockwood, Beatrix, and Annaliese Griffin. "The System: The Ins and Outs of Bail." The Marshall Project, Oct. 28, 2020, https://www.themarshallproject.org/2020/10/28/the-ins-and-outs-of-bail.

Burdens low-income women Ibid.

Chanta Parker "End Bail Money Now!" Essie Justice Group, YouTube.com, May 2, 2017, accessed Feb. 23, 2023, https://www.youtube.com/watch?v=7lYvH1bAObU.

Maximizing at justice's expense Preston, Allie. "Fact Sheet: Profit over People: Inside the Commercial Bail Bond Industry Fueling America's Cash Bail Systems." Center for American Progress, July 13, 2022, https://www.americanprogress.org/article/fact-sheet-profit-over-people/.

Underwritten bail bonds Preston, Allie, and Eisenberg, Rachel. "Profit over People: Inside the Commercial Bail Bond Industry Fueling America's Cash Bail Systems." Center for American Progress, July 6, 2022, https://www.americanprogress.org/article/profit-over-people/.

$2.4 billion profit annually Preston, Allie. "Fact Sheet: Profit over People: Inside the Commercial Bail Bond Industry Fueling America's Cash Bail Systems." Center for American Progress, July 13, 2022, https://www.americanprogress.org/article/fact-sheet-profit-over-people/.

Harms white people, too Wertz, J., D. Azrael, J. Berrigan, et al. "A Typology of Civilians Shot and Killed by US Police—a Latent Class Analysis of Firearm Legal Intervention Homicide in the 2014–2015 National Violent Death Reporting System." *Journal of Urban Health*, no. 97 (2020), pp. 317–28, https://doi.org/10.1007/s11524-020-00430-0. Even though Black people are still two times more likely to be killed by police than whites, white people still make up 54 percent of those who die in police encounters—that's nothing to make light of.

Abolition of debt Valdez, Jonah. "Nearly $4 Billion in Federal Student Loan Debt Canceled for Former ITT Tech Students." *Los Angeles Times*, Aug. 17, 2022, https://www.latimes.com/world-nation/story/2022-08-16/itt-tech-federal-student-loan-debt-canceled.

Post office financial services Baradaran, Mehrsa. "It's Time for Postal Banking." *Harvard Law Review*, Feb. 24, 2014, https://harvardlawreview.org/2014/02/its-time-for-postal-banking/#_ftnref2.

How USPS could do it "Providing Non-Bank Financial Services for the Underserved." Risk Analysis Research Center, United States Postal Service Office of Inspector General, Jan. 27, 2014, https://www.uspsoig.gov/sites/default/files/reports/2023-01/rarc-wp-11-007_0_0.pdf.

Corinthian College debt cancellation "Corinthian Strike Team Demands Debt Cancellation in Washington DC." *Power Report*, The Debt Collective, Apr. 1, 2015, https://powerreport.debtcollective.org/reports/2015-3-1-corinthian-100-demanding-debt-cancellation-in-washington-dc/.

"Education Department Approves $5.8 Billion Group Discharge to Cancel All Remaining Loans for 560,000 Borrowers Who Attended Corinthian." U.S. Department of Education, June 1, 2022, https://www.ed.gov/news/press-releases/education-department-approves-58-billion-group-discharge-cancel-all-remaining-loans-560000-borrowers-who-attended-corinthian-colleges.

CHAPTER 8.

Heating since industrial revolution Braam, Anna. "Review: Ian Gough: Heat, Greed and Human Need—Climate Change, Capitalism and Sustainable Wellbeing." *Intergenerational Justice Review*, DEU, Feb. 2018, https://nbn-resolving.org/urn:nbn:de:0168-ssoar-61326-4.

Satgar, Vishwas. "The Climate Crisis and Systemic Alternatives." *Climate Crisis: South African and Global Democratic Eco-Socialist Alternatives*, Johannesburg, South Africa: Wits University Press, 2018.

Rising sea levels Ibid.

Global south vulnerability Althor, Glenn, et al. "Global Mismatch between Greenhouse Gas Emissions and the Burden of Climate Change." *Nature News*, Nature Publishing Group, Feb. 5, 2016, https://www.nature.com/articles/srep20281.

Heat-related deaths Lieberman, Bruce. "1.5 Or 2 Degrees Celsius of Additional Global Warming: Does It Make a Difference?" *Yale Climate Connections*, Aug. 4, 2021, https://yaleclimateconnections.org/2021/08/1-5-or-2-degrees-celsius-of-additional-global-warming-does-it-make-a-difference/.

Air pollution economic damage Goodkind, Andrew L., et al. "Fine-Scale Damage Estimates of Particulate Matter Air Pollution Reveal Opportunities for Location-Specific Mitigation of Emissions." *Proceedings of the National Academy of Sciences*, vol. 116, no. 18 (2019), pp. 8775–80, https://doi.org/10.1073/pnas.1816102116.

Clean energy savings Kirk, Karin. "The Number of Lives That Clean Energy Could Save, by U.S. State." *Yale Climate Connections*, July 14, 2021, https://yaleclimateconnections.org/2021/07/the-number-of-lives-that-clean-energy-could-save-by-u-s-state/.

What capitalists do Li, Mei, et al. "The Clean Energy Claims of BP, Chevron, Exxon-Mobil and Shell: A Mismatch between Discourse, Actions and Investments." PLOS ONE, Public Library of Science, Feb. 16, 2022, https://journals.plos.org/plosone/article/authors?id=10.1371%2Fjournal.pone.0263596.

Accusations of greenwashing Ibid.

"Advance cleaner fuels" Sommers, Mike. "Mike Sommers (@mj_sommers) / Twitter." Twitter.com, Sept. 30, 2010, available at https://web.archive.org/web/20220526223513/https://twitter.com/mj_sommers.

InfluenceMap "Climate Change and Digital Advertising: The Oil & Gas Sector's Digital Advertising Strategy." *InfluenceMap*, Aug. 2021, https://pedlowski.files.wordpress.com/2021/08/influencemap_climatechangedigitaladvertisingreport_august2021.pdf.

Increase clean energy Tabuchi, Hiroko. "Oil Producers Used Facebook to Counter President Biden's Clean Energy Message, a Study Shows." *New York Times*, Aug. 5, 2021, https://www.nytimes.com/2021/08/05/climate/oil-facebook-ads-biden.html.

Californians for Energy Independence Borgeson, Merrian. "Unmasked: The Oil Industry Campaign to Undermine California's Clean Energy Future." National Resources Defense Council, Nov. 6, 2014, https://www.nrdc.org/experts/merrian-borgeson/unmasked-oil-industry-campaign-undermine-californias-clean-energy-future.

Over $55 million Rowland-Shea, Jenny, and Zainab Mirza. "How Oil Lobbyists Use a Rigged System to Hamstring Biden's Climate Agenda." Center for American Progress, Sept. 30, 2021, https://www.americanprogress.org/article/oil-lobbyists-use-rigged-system-hamstring-bidens-climate-agenda/.

$13.4 million from oil and gas Zibel, Alan. "Big Oil's Capitol Hill Allies." Public Citizen, Feb. 10, 2021, https://www.citizen.org/article/big-oils-capitol-hill-allies/.

Playing footsie with oil Flavelle, Christopher, et al. "How Joe Manchin Aided Coal, and Earned Millions." *New York Times*, Mar. 27, 2022, https://www.nytimes.com/2022/03/27/climate/manchin-coal-climate-conflicts.html.

Unlikely any time soon Gore, D'Angelo. "Examining U.S. 'Energy Independence' Claims." FactCheck.org, Mar. 9, 2022, https://www.factcheck.org/2022/03/examining-u-s-energy-independence-claims/.

Disproportionately white males Brady, Jeff. "Big Oil Has a Diversity Problem." NPR, Nov. 5, 2017, https://www.npr.org/2017/11/05/553969144/big-oil-has-a-diversity-problem.

Harder, Amy. "Civil Rights Leaders Call for More Diverse Oil and Gas Industry." *Axios*, June 8, 2020, https://www.axios.com/2020/06/08/oil-gas-industry-diversity.

Drilling in minority communities Fears, Darryl. "Black, Latino Communities Have a Higher Level of Oil Drilling and Pollution." *Washington Post*, Apr. 18, 2022, https://www.washingtonpost.com/nation/2022/04/15/redlined-oil-drilling-pollution-study/.

Citing job losses Bedayn, Jesse. "'Just Transition' Bill for Oil Industry Workers

Exposes Labor Rift." *CalMatters*, Feb. 17, 2022, https://calmatters.org/california-divide/2022/02/just-transition-bill-for-oil-industry-workers-exposes-labor-rift/.

Environmental groups warned   "Briefing: U.S. Oil and Gas Companies Set to Make Tens of Billions More from Wartime Oil Prices in 2022." *Greenpeace USA*, Mar. 29, 2022, https://www.greenpeace.org/usa/research/briefing-u-s-oil-and-gas-companies-set-to-make-tens-of-billions-more-from-wartime-oil-prices-in-2022/.

"Separation of oil and state"   Ibid.

"A commitment to safe climate"   Baer, Hans. "Afterword: Toward Eco-Socialism as a Global and Local Strategy to Cool Down the World-System." *Cooling Down: Local Responses to Global Climate Change*, New York: Berghan Books, 2022, pp. 368–69.

Reliance on fossil fuels   Mann, Michael E. "Individual Choices Won't Be Enough to Save the Planet." *Time*, Sept. 12, 2019, https://time.com/5669071/lifestyle-changes-climate-change/.

Federal fuel consumption   Weisbrod, Katelyn. "The U.S. Military Emits More Carbon Dioxide into the Atmosphere than Entire Countries like Denmark or Portugal." *Inside Climate News*, Jan. 12, 2022, https://insideclimatenews.org/news/18012022/military-carbon-emissions/#:~:text=Using%20Department%20of%20Energy%20data,metric%20tons%20of%20greenhouse%20gases.

Destruction of conditions for life   Brundenius, Claes. *Reflections on Socialism in the Twenty-First Century: Facing Market Liberalism, Rising Inequalities and the Environmental Imperative*, New York: Springer, 2020.

Form sustainable cooperatives   "Sustainable Communities Initiative." Cooperation Jackson, https://cooperationjackson.org/sustainable-communities-initiative.

CHAPTER 9.

Club for Growth action   "Top Organizations Disclosing Donations to Club for Growth Action, 2022." OpenSecrets.org, 2022, https://www.opensecrets.org/outside-spending/detail/2022?cmte=C00487470&tab=donors.

"Top Organizations Disclosing Donations to Club for Growth Action, 2020." OpenSecrets.org, 2020, https://www.opensecrets.org/outside-spending/detail/2020?cmte=C00487470&tab=donors.

"Top Organizations Disclosing Donations to Club for Growth Action, 2018." OpenSecrets.org, 2018, https://www.opensecrets.org/outside-spending/detail/2018?cmte=C00487470&tab=donors.

"Top Organizations Disclosing Donations to Club for Growth Action, 2016." OpenSecrets.org, 2016, https://www.opensecrets.org/outside-spending/detail/2016?cmte=C00487470&tab=donors.

Mission statement   "Club for Growth Action: Conservative Super PAC." Club for Growth, Feb. 9, 2023, https://www.clubforgrowth.org/about/club-for-growth-action/.

Jeff Yass   "Profile: Jeff Yass." *Forbes*, Feb. 24, 2023, https://www.forbes.com/profile/jeff-yass/?sh=4cff49355f1a.

Smattering of Democrats   "Susquehanna International Group Profile: Recipients." OpenSecrets.org, 2022, https://www.opensecrets.org/orgs/susquehanna-international-group/recipients?id=D000030211.

Cofounded the PAC Caruso, Stephen. "Pa.'s Richest Person Has Spent at Least $18 Million on the 2022 Primary—Mostly to Influence One Issue." *Spotlight PA*, May 16, 2022, https://www.spotlightpa.org/news/2022/05/pa-primary-2022-billionaire-donations-jeff-yass/.

Commonwealth Children's Choice Fund "Commonwealth Children's Choice Fund Campaign Finance Profile." Campaign Finance Online Filing, Pennsylvania Department of State, https://www.campaignfinanceonline.pa.gov/Pages/CFAnnualTotals.aspx?Filer=20190183.

Scott Martin "PA Senate Education Committee Vote: Sen. Scott Martin Proposes Largest Transfer of Taxpayer Dollars out of Public Schools in PA History." Pennsylvania State Education Association, June 7, 2021, https://www.psea.org/news--events/newsstand/press-center/news-release---june-7-2021/.

Willie Horton Johnson, Dennis W. *Democracy for Hire: A History of American Political Consulting*, New York: Oxford University Press, 2017, p. 272.

Misleadingly stoke racial fears Jamieson, Kathleen Hall, Ph.D. "Professor: Political Ads Ripe with Deception," *The Daily Pennsylvanian*, Nov. 3, 2005, https://www.thedp.com/article/2005/11/professor_political_ads_rife_with_deception.

Increasingly pouring into campaigns Sultan, Niv M. "Election 2016: Trump's Free Media Helped Keep Cost Down." *OpenSecrets News*, Apr. 13, 2017, https://www.opensecrets.org/news/2017/04/election-2016-trump-fewer-donors-provided-more-of-the-cash/.

Larger campaign contributions Lau, Tim. "Citizens United Explained." Brennan Center for Justice, Dec. 12, 2019, https://www.brennancenter.org/our-work/research-reports/citizens-united-explained.

Dark money Torres-Spelliscy, Ciara. "Dark Money in the 2020 Election." Brennan Center for Justice, Nov. 20, 2020, https://www.brennancenter.org/our-work/analysis-opinion/dark-money-2020-election.

Dark money 2020 election Gude, Shawn. "The Folly of Campaign Finance Reform: To Citizens United v. FEC, Add McCutcheon v. FEC." Democratic Socialists of America, Apr. 16, 2014, https://www.dsausa.org/democratic-left/the_folly_of_campaign_finance_reform-2/.

$1 billion on 2020 elections "2020 Outside Spending, by Super PAC," OpenSecrets.org, https://www.opensecrets.org/outside-spending/super_pacs/2020?chart=V&disp=O&type=S. The top five Super PACs spent $903.73 million.

Lobbying can work Showalter, Reed. "Democracy for Sale: Examining the Effects of Concentration on Lobbying in the United States." American Economic Liberties Project, Aug. 25, 2021, https://www.economicliberties.us/our-work/democracy-for-sale/#_ftnref1.

Higher return on equity Kim, Jin-Hyuk. "Corporate Lobbying Revisited—LMU." *Munich Personal RePEc Archive*, 2008, https://mpra.ub.uni-muenchen.de/51396/1/MPRA_paper_51396.pdf.

Shaffer, Brian, et al. "Firm Level Performance Implications of Nonmarket Actions." *Business & Society*, vol. 39, no. 2 (2000), pp. 126–43, https://doi.org/10.1177/000765030003900202.

Corporate influence on democracy Matthews, Dylan. "Remember That Study Saying

America Is an Oligarchy? 3 Rebuttals Say It's Wrong." *Vox*, May 9, 2016, https://www.vox.com/2016/5/9/11502464/gilens-page-oligarchy-study.

Total policy impact Savage, Luke. "Campaign Finance Reform by Itself Won't End Elite Control of Politics." *Jacobin*, Mar. 22, 2021, https://jacobin.com/2021/03/campaign-finance-reform-canada-united-states-politics.

Woll, Cornelia. "Corporate Power beyond Lobbying." *American Affairs Journal*, Sept. 12, 2019, https://americanaffairsjournal.org/2019/08/corporate-power-beyond-lobbying/.

Matches eightfold "How It Works." New York City Campaign Finance Board, https://www.nyccfb.info/program/how-it-works.

Established program already "Public Funding of Presidential Elections." Federal Election Commission, https://www.fec.gov/introduction-campaign-finance/understanding-ways-support-federal-candidates/presidential-elections/public-funding-presidential-elections/.

Qualifying candidates participated Weiser, Wendy R., and Alicia Bannon. "Democracy: An Election Agenda for Candidates, Activists, and Legislators." Brennan Center for Justice, May 4, 2018, https://www.brennancenter.org/our-work/policy-solutions/democracy-election-agenda-candidates-activists-and-legislators

After inadequate funding Ibid.

600 percent matching funds Price, David E. "H.R.3955—115th Congress (2017–2018): Empowering Citizens Act of 2017 . . ." Library of Congress, 2017, https://www.congress.gov/bill/115th-congress/house-bill/3955.

One45 project Long, Ariama C. "Richardson-Jordan, Barron on one45 Project Withdrawal in Harlem." *New York Amsterdam News*, June 9, 2022, https://amsterdamnews.com/news/2022/06/09/richardson-jordan-barron-on-one45-project-withdrawal-in-harlem/.

David Zapolsky Blest, Paul. "Leaked Amazon Memo Details Plan to Smear Fired Warehouse Organizer: 'He's Not Smart or Articulate.'" VICE, Apr. 2, 2020, https://www.vice.com/en/article/5dm8bx/leaked-amazon-memo-details-plan-to-smear-fired-warehouse-organizer-hes-not-smart-or-articulate.

Win election to unionize McAlevey, Jane. "The Amazon Labor Union's Historic Victory Was the First Step." *The Nation*, Apr. 15, 2022, https://www.thenation.com/article/society/amazon-union-vote-staten-island/.

List of unions "Labor Movement Relief Funds: AFL-CIO." AFL-CIO, 2023, https://afl-cio.org/covid-19/labor-movement-relief-funds.

Negotiate a successful contract "Dolores Huerta." *Archives of Women's Political Communication*, Iowa State University, 2023, https://awpc.cattcenter.iastate.edu/directory/dolores-huerta/.

About the Creators

Malaika Jabali is the Senior News and Politics Editor at *Essence* magazine. Her writing has appeared in *The Root*, *Teen Vogue*, the *New Republic*, and *The Guardian*, where she was a columnist. She received her JD from Columbia University Law School, where she was an articles editor for the *Columbia Journal of Race and Law*, and her MS from the Columbia School of Social Work. Her political feature "The Color of Economic Anxiety" won the 2019 New York Association for Black Journalists  award for magazine feature. She is a licensed attorney who has written laws and worked in housing policy for the New York City Council and the former co-chair of Operation P.O.W.E.R., a grassroots organization focused on bringing Black radical politics to New York City. She is also a survivor of NYC's dating scene, so, fortunately for readers (but unfortunately for her), she has *plenty* of experience with leaving toxic situations behind.

Kayla E. is a Texas-born artist and designer of Mexican American descent. She earned her BA from Harvard University, where she was awarded the Albert Alcalay Prize in and served as art director for the *Harvard Lampoon*. For nearly a decade, she was the editor-in-chief of *Nat. Brut*, an art and literary magazine. Kayla is the recipient of a Princeton Hodder Fellowship, which aided in the completion of *Precious Rubbish*, her upcoming graphic memoir about a childhood disorganized by intrafamilial abuse, addiction, and sexual violence. Kayla lives in rural North Carolina with her wife, Laura Bullard, and works as the creative director at Fantagraphics. Find her online at kaylaework.com.